The God of Creation
Truth and Gospel in Genesis

Richard D Phillips

EP BOOKS

1st Floor Venture House, 6 Silver Court, Watchmead,
Welwyn Garden City, UK, AL7 1TS

www.epbooks.org
sales@epbooks.org

EP Books are distributed in the USA by:
JPL Distribution
3741 Linden Avenue Southeast
Grand Rapids, MI 49548

www.jplbooks.com
orders@jplbooks.com

First published 2018

British Library Cataloguing in Publication Data available

ISBN 978-1-78397-220-3

To Harry L. Reeder, III

with thanks to God for his friendship and ministry

and

to the Word

who in the beginning was God, was with God, and

through whom all things were made (John 1:1–3)

Commendations

Richard D. Phillips' *The God of Creation* defends a faithful reading of Genesis 1:1–2:3 as historical narrative, and explains why other interpretive schemes (such as the gap theory, day-age theory and framework hypothesis) should be rejected. He encourages the reader to value science while not elevating it to an unwarranted position of authority over Scripture. But he also lifts our eyes to more expansive horizons by offering us a Christ-centered, gospel-focused and devotional exposition of what this passage teaches us concerning God, ourselves and the world around us. We discover afresh how deeply relevant the first book of the Bible is, as it challenges today's popular philosophies and idolatries.

Paul Garner BSc, MSc, FGS, Researcher and Lecturer for Biblical Creation Trust. His MSc is in Geoscience (specialising in palaeobiology) from University College London. He is a member of several scientific societies. His first book, *The New Creationism: Building Scientific Theories on a Biblical Foundation*, is published by EP Books.

"A massively important and popular approach to the multiple issues surrounding the creation narratives in Genesis that divide Christians and secularists and often divide Christians too. Philips has a point of view (of course, why else would one write a book?) and he makes what is perhaps the best and most convincing case for it. And what is his point of view? Read the book and find out. Even if you disagree, you will need hefty arguments to refute what Philips defends here. A most welcome addition to the challenge of Genesis 1 and 2 in a secular world."

Derek W. H. Thomas
Senior Minister, First Presbyterian Church, Columbia SC
Chancellor's Professor, Reformed Theological Seminary
Teaching Fellow, Ligonier Ministries

Contents

About the Author

Richard Davis Phillips has been the Senior Minister of Second Presbyterian Church in Greenville, South Carolina (Presbyterian Church of America) since July, 2007. Prior to entering the ministry, he commanded tank units as an officer in the U.S. Army and later served as an assistant professor of leadership at the U.S. Military Academy at West Point. He came to faith in Jesus Christ at the age of 30, and was soon leading evangelistic Bible studies at the college where he was teaching. A few years later he received God's call to enter the gospel ministry, and received a Master of Divinity degree from Westminster Theological Seminary in Philadelphia, PA.

After graduation he joined the pastoral staff of the church where he came to faith, Tenth Presbyterian Church of Philadelphia, PA. There, Rick was mentored by the well-known Bible teacher, Dr James Montgomery Boice, and began his calling as a weekly preacher of God's Word. After serving at Tenth Presbyterian from 1995–2002, Dr Phillips accepted the call to be Senior Minister of First Presbyterian Church of Margate, FL. After five years there, he moved to Greenville.

Dr Phillips describes his ministry as centring on three "P"s: preaching, praying, and pastoring. He is devoted to expository preaching, which is the teaching of whole books of the Bible week-by-week. His ministry is widely heard on the radio and the internet and Dr Phillips is frequently called upon to speak at conferences on the Bible and Reformed theology. He further serves the church by authoring books, with over twenty-five currently in print. Among his many activities, he serves on the board and council of the Alliance of Confessing Evangelicals, the council of The Gospel Coalition, and the board of trustees of Westminster Theological Seminary. He is Chairman of the Philadelphia Conference on Reformed Theology. Together with Philip Graham Ryken, he is series co-editor of the Reformed Expository Commentary series. In addition to the Master of Divinity degree from Westminster Theological Theological Seminary, Dr Phillips holds degrees from Greenville Presbyterian Theological Seminary (Doctor of Divinity), the University of Pennsylvania (M.B.A.) and the University of Michigan (B.A.).

Rick is married to the former Sharon Wilkey, whom he met at church in Philadelphia. Sharon is a homemaker, author, and home-schooling mother. They have an active family of five children: Hannah, Matthew, Jonathan, Ellie and Lydia.

I   *In the Beginning*

Genesis 1:1

In the beginning, God created the heavens and the earth
(Genesis 1:1).

WHAT DIFFERENCE DOES THE DOCTRINE OF CREATION MAKE?
According to the apostle Paul, creation makes a lot of
difference! It is not by chance that when Paul began his long
exposition of the gospel in the book of Romans, he began
with God as the Creator. Why is everyone accountable to
believe in God? Paul answers, since "what can be known
about God is plain to them, because God has shown it to
them" (Romans 1:19). But when did God reveal himself
to every person? Paul replies, "ever since the creation of
the world in the things that have been made" (Romans
1:20). Creation matters! Because God is first and foremost
our Creator.

Man's big problem is that he forgets about God. One great
remedy is the creation that surrounds us. Seldom has the
impact of God's creation been more potently stated than on
Christmas Eve, 1968, as the *Apollo 8* spacecraft orbited the
moon for the first time ever. Never before had human eyes
beheld the planet Earth rising above the surface of another
sphere. The world held its breath at the images beaming back

from the lunar capsule window and the broadcasters were literally speechless. What do you say in response to the first view of our planet rising over an alien horizon? Astronaut William Anders knew, breaking the silence in the crackling hiss of the distant radio with the words of Genesis 1:1: "In the beginning, God created the heavens and the earth."[1] In this way, the marveling human race fulfilled the purpose of creation by giving glory to God!

The Beginning of All Things

Little children ask, "Mommy, where did we come from?" Even at a young age we realize that our origins say much about who we are. In its opening sentence, Genesis answers this important question.

It is from this opening statement—actually, from its very first word—that the Bible's first book receives its name. The Latin word for "In the beginning," is *Genesis*. This is a fitting title, because Genesis is the book of origins. Here we learn about the beginning of the universe and of history. If we want to understand the world, the meaning of life, the nature of our own selves, the salvation for which we hope, and the destiny awaiting us in the end, the origin of all these things are recorded in Genesis.

These words, "In the beginning," form the initial basis for a Christian worldview. That there was a beginning means that things have not always been. Matter and life had a definite start, and by identifying that origin we learn vital truths about them.

In the 1950s, scientists taught a "steady-state" theory of the universe, stating that it has always existed. This theory needed to be replaced when Edwin Hubble observed that the stars and galaxies are moving apart from one another, evidence which suggests that there was a beginning which launched this matter into all directions. The currently dominant scientific theory is therefore called the "Big Bang," which supposedly took place some 13.7 billion years ago. This idea holds that first there was nothing, then there was an explosion (or a "singularity" as it is sometimes called) that caused everything. The Big Bang theory leaves numerous questions unanswered, most important of which is the question of origins. If the universe started with the Big Bang, we inevitably ask, "What caused the Big Bang?" Moreover, we ask, how is it rational to believe that something came from nothing? If you can believe that something came from nothing, the Christian asks the secularist, please do not complain about the supposed irrationality of the resurrection of Jesus!

Genesis 1:1 agrees with the Big Bang Theory in that there was a beginning to the universe, even if it radically disagrees on the source of that beginning. Even this agreement is worth something, since the idea of a beginning rejects the circular idea of history common to Eastern religions and so popular in our culture today. If there was a beginning, then history really is not a never-ending circle. If there was a point where everything began, then things have not always been. Time is not a circle, but a trajectory. We may therefore ask where the line is pointing. Before we see what the answer is, the question itself is important. If there is a beginning, there is history, meaning, direction, and purpose. We are already on our way to a Christian worldview! What, then, is the source of this beginning, and therefore of history and meaning?

God in the Beginning

"In the beginning," says Genesis 1:1, prompting a question: "Yes, so what was in the beginning?" It immediately answers, "God." Here we confront one of the most titanic claims in the entire Bible. If there was a beginning, what was already there at the beginning? The Scriptures answer, "God was there." "The cause of everything that is, [Genesis] says, is the creative, powerful, and sovereign hand of almighty God."[2] Here is the great truth claim on which all that follows in the Christian faith proceeds: God is our Creator.

Christians disagree with secular science on the source of the beginning. This difference stems from the fact that the Bible gives an answer whereas science does not. We ask, what was the true and first cause of all that there is? Science has no answer. There was a "singularity," secularism mutters vaguely. So what caused the singularity? Only silence is heard. This is not because scientists are not smart. It is rather because science begins with a presupposition of *materialism*. Science does not prove that all reality takes the form of matter, but rather assumes it. Science builds on observable, material causes, presupposing that nothing else exists.

Christianity is a worldview that wants to challenge the scientific assumption of materialism. Ravi Zacharias has said that we live in "an 'ontologically haunted' universe," meaning that observable reality cannot provide an answer for its being. Thus, where science surrenders in silence on the question of origins, the Christian faith points to an *immaterial* source. Zacharias writes: "There has to be something more than physical or 'natural,' something quite different in character from which or from whom this physical universe derives its existence."³ On this rationale, Christians urge secularists to consider the possibility of a personal, non-material source for all things, namely, Genesis 1:1's claim: "In the beginning, God."

Science replies, "So tell us where God came from?" Here, Christians agree that there is ultimate mystery at the beginning. But Christians differ from science in that our position is not absurd. Science declares that everything came from nothing—an objectively irrational claim. Christians say that everything came from Someone—a mystery, for sure, but not an irrational one.

The Bible's first verse claims that there is a single being who does not have a beginning: God. In the beginning, God already was. God is the actor in creation and is the source of all things. This statement is staggering in its implications. We earlier noted that a beginning indicates a direction and future. Since the beginning indicates a trajectory, if God was in the beginning then he created not only the beginning but determined its direction. If the cause and source of history is a person, as the Bible says, then the purpose of creation and the meaning of life is shaped by the mind and will of him who made it all. Already in Genesis 1:1, therefore, we encounter the reality that Moses put so beautifully in Psalm 90:

> Before the mountains were brought forth, or ever you had formed the earth and the world, from everlasting to everlasting you are God (Psalm 90:2).

Genesis 1:1 declares God not only as the source of all things but as the subject of the Bible that will follow. G. C. Aalders writes: "The first words of Scripture purposely lift our hearts on high to God. In this way it becomes apparent from the outset that Holy Scripture, in its very nature, is the revelation of God. And first of all, the revelation of God as Creator."[4]

If in the beginning God already was, then God is not himself a part of the creation. Look at all the worldview packed into Genesis 1:1! Here, it stands against *pantheism*, the popular view that "God is all and all is God." Instead, the Bible says there is God the Creator and there is the creation. They are not one and the same. God is apart from his creation. His being exists outside of the rocks, rivers and trees. Neither is he like the mythological gods of ancient Babylon and Greece, whose soap-opera existence is a reflection of human foibles. The world with all the things in it is not eternal but is created. God alone is eternal, absolutely free above all that is.

Reading that God was in the beginning provides the greatest comfort to the believer, especially when he or she prays to God in time of need. God is involved and invested in the creation, otherwise we would not have Genesis 1:1. At the same time, God is exalted above the creation. He who was before is also after and above. His will, which formed the universe, is not constrained by any created power. This realization grounded the hope of Psalm 121:

> I lift up my eyes to the hills. From where does my help come? My help comes from the Lord, who made heaven and earth" (Psalm 121:1–2).

The Creator's help is one that cannot be thwarted by anything in this world. Paul likewise grounds his salvation hope in God's supremacy over all creation: "For I am sure that neither death nor life, nor angels nor rulers, nor things present nor things to come, nor powers, nor height nor depth, nor anything else in all creation, will be able to separate us from the love of God in Christ Jesus our Lord" (Romans 8:38–39).

More broadly, in this opening verse, the aim of the entire Bible is disclosed. "In the beginning, God" means that there is a personal source who has determined the purpose and direction of all things. It raises the question, "What is your relationship to God? Do you know him? Do you know his purpose for you and your life? Do you know how to be in his favor?" G. Campbell Morgan observes:

> God is the originating Cause; man is His stuff, His design, His workmanship. These are the things from which I cannot escape. I live and move and have my being in Him, whether I will or not; the beating of my heart, the throbbing of my nerves, all these things are of Him.[5]

Created in the Beginning

The final statement of Genesis 1:1 is that in the beginning God "created the heavens and the earth." The word used for "create" (Hebrew, *bara*) is a seldom-used term that always refers to God's activity in making things from nothing. Alec Motyer writes that when this verb *to create* "has a subject, it is always God; when it has a presumed subjected, it is always God ... it is used throughout the Old Testament of acts or events which either by their specialty or novelty or both point to God as their originator."[6] In Genesis 1, this word is used only three times: in verse 1 for the creation of all things, in verse 21 when God created the living creatures, and in verse 27 when God created man in his own image.

This means that Genesis 1:1 describes creation as *ex nihilo*, out of nothing. Christians do not believe the absurd proposition that something came from nothing. We believe that God, who has always been, created all things where there had been nothing but himself. Only God can create in this way, never man. The distinction is between making things out of existing material, as for instance a carpenter making a chair, and that of creating the wood itself that will become the chair. The New Testament identifies creation *ex nihilo* as a cardinal doctrine of the Christian faith: "By faith we understand that the universe was created by the word of God, so that what is seen was not made out of things that are visible" (Hebrews 11:3).

It is awesome to consider the universe that God created by his own power. Physicist Stephen Hawking stated in his best-selling book *A Brief History of Time* that our galaxy is of only average size at a diameter of 100,000 light-years. "Our galaxy is only one of some hundred thousand million that can be seen using modern telescopes, each galaxy itself containing some hundred thousand million stars."[7] Pulling out our microscopes, Genesis 1:1 challenges us to consider that God created ever molecule in all those hundred thousand million galaxies. R. Kent Hughes writes: "He created every atom—the sub-microscopic solar systems with the whimsically named quarks ... and leptons ... and electrons and neutrinos ... all of which have no measurable size."[8] To consider the magnitude and the marvel of what God has created is to stand in awe of his glory, power, and wisdom. Instead of shrinking back from the claim that a single deity created all those stars and galaxies, composed of so vast a number of atoms and molecules,

Christians embrace that claim as a cause to marvel in God's praise. This is, in fact, exactly what the biblical writers did:

> To whom then will you compare me, that I should be like him? says the Holy One. Lift up your eyes on high and see: who created these? He who brings out their host by number, calling them all by name, by the greatness of his might, and because he is strong in power not one is missing (Isaiah 40:25–26).

To say that God created all things rules out the theory that matter came into being by chance. Instead, Genesis 1:1 launches a highly developed creative process that shaped and formed all things. Therefore, not only broad categories like matter and time were created by God, but actual planets, molecules, laws of nature, and definitions of life. What God created, he also formed. This is true not only for physical laws but also for moral laws. The Ten Commandments are just as fixedly created as are the laws of nature.

Realizing God's created design is increasingly essential in today's neo-pagan Western culture. We hear that gender is a social construct, whereas Genesis says that God created man "male and female" (Genesis 1:27). Our courts may decree that marriage licenses must be issued to any kind of romantic relationship, but Genesis 2 will teach that God created marriage between a man and a woman. There is right and wrong, life and death, male and female, good and evil because of God's sovereign design in creation. We may reject these created distinctions not only to our peril but to the great offense of the living God who created them as a reflection of his own glorious character.

It is in this sense that Genesis 1:1 was written as a frontal assault against the worldly tendency to idolatry. The original readers of Genesis lived in a world where idolatry was common and widespread, just as we do today. Contemporary men and women may not bow to idols of wood and stone, but they just as surely worship the gods of gold, silicon, and sex. And this is what Genesis 1 confronts! "In the beginning, God" is an assault against all false gods and all false worship. Henri Blocher writes: "Just as Abraham left his family and the land of his ancestors, so with its very first step the metaphysics of the Bible leaves behind the metaphysics of the pagan world."[9] There is one God who in the beginning created the heavens and the earth. Genesis declares that the maker of the galaxies is the God of Abraham, Isaac, and Jacob, the God who revealed himself not only in creation but also through his revealed Word in Holy Scripture. Rebellious creatures who refuse him worship and exalt others in his place will find themselves at odds with the very Creator whose purposes are certain to stand.

A Story Begins

The words, "In the beginning," point to a history that began long ago and of which we are still a part. There is a trajectory and a story that Genesis 1:1 announces. The great question to ask is "What is that story?" If we wonder, we should ask the original audience to whom the book of Genesis was written. The Bible tells us that Genesis was written by Moses during the time of Israel's exodus from Egypt. Therefore, when we read the words, "In the beginning, God created the heavens and the earth," we should imagine the people of Israel walking on the desert earth, gazing up at the million shining lights of the blazing heavens which God had made. God created all the glory shining down on them, as well as the good earth of the land to which they were sojourning. If we ask those Israelite readers, "What is your story?" we will gain a clue to what began in Genesis 1:1.

Their answer is that the story that began with God's creation has become the great story of God's redemption. They were experiencing deliverance from bondage into freedom, and redemption to a land which God had promised. This is what God was beginning in the Bible's first verse! Their story looked back to God's creation and then to man's sin and the misery and death it produced. But their story looked forward to a Savior, who was also part of God's original design.

It is no wonder, then, that the Christian message begins in language that deliberately echoes Genesis 1:1. Whereas Moses began the Bible, "In the beginning, God created the heavens and the earth," the apostle John began his Gospel, speaking of Jesus Christ: "In the beginning was the Word" (John 1:1).

In this way we are reminded that to begin the Bible is to relish the story it tells, the terrible problem it defines, and the marvelous solution it offers from God. Just as the Israelites who first heard the message of Genesis were a people moving forward to a saving encounter with God's Messiah, so too should we read Genesis as a beginning of our meeting with God. History's story has a beginning! But it also has an end in the Savior God prepared to meet us in our greatest need, the Redeemer Jesus Christ, who forgives us of our sin.

2   *Introducing ... God*

In the beginning, God ... (Genesis 1:1).

DURING THE YEARS 1642–1649, A GROUP OF LEADING theologians (known as "divines") met in Westminster Abbey to devise a doctrinal statement for England. The result was the *Westminster Confession of Faith*, with its Shorter and Larger Catechisms. The character of the Westminster Assembly is indicated by how they approached the second question of their Shorter Catechism, which asked the question, "What is God?" Historian William Hetherington relates that "each man felt the unapproachable sublimity of the divine idea suggested by these words. ... All shrunk from the too sacred task in awestruck, reverential fear."[10] The suggestion was made to show humility by having the youngest member present to offer his view first. This younger minister declined, but when pressed he asked permission to pray aloud. Hetherington reports: "Then in slow and solemn accents he thus began his prayer: 'O God, thou art a spirit, infinite, eternal, and unchangeable, in thy being, wisdom, power, holiness, justice, goodness, and truth.' When he ceased, the first sentence of his prayer was immediately written by one of the brethren, read, and adopted, as the most perfect answer that could be conceived, as, indeed, in a very sacred sense, God's own answer."[11]

On Knowing God

This vignette illustrates two vital points about the knowledge of God. The first point is that knowing God is the highest endeavor of mankind. We can see this when we open our Bible and turn to its first words: "In the beginning, God." Set before us is the great subject of the entire Bible and all of life. Jesus stated: "this is eternal life, that they may know you the only true God" (John 17:1). When the Scriptures take us back to the beginning we find that God is there. In the first thing that happens in all of history, God is the actor; in Genesis 1:1, God is the subject who goes with the first verb, telling us that he "created."

At the very heart of a Christian worldview is the knowledge of God. Charles Spurgeon emphasized this priority in the very first sermon of his historic 38-year ministry in London. In 1854, the 19 year-old Spurgeon declared the central importance of knowing God:

> The highest science, the loftiest speculation, the mightiest philosophy, which can ever engage the attention of a child of God, is the name, the nature, the person, the work, the doings, and the existence of the great God whom he calls his Father ... It is a subject so vast, that all our thoughts are lost in its immensity; so deep, that our pride is drowned in its infinity ... Nothing will so enlarge the intellect, nothing so magnify the whole soul of man, as a devout, earnest, continued investigation of the great subject of the Deity.[12]

It is little wonder that, springing from these opening words, Spurgeon's ministry would be so remarkably blessed by God's power.

While Spurgeon points out the value of studying God, theologian J. I. Packer notes the peril to those who neglect to know God:

> The world becomes a strange, mad, painful place, and life in it a disappointing and unpleasant business ... Disregard the study of God, and you sentence yourself to stumble and blunder through life blindfold, as it were, with no sense of direction and no understanding of what surrounds you. This way you can waste your life and lose your soul.[13]

This being the case, whenever we study the Bible, whether in the church, in a small group, or privately, the one question we must always ask is, "What does this teaching tell me about God?" As we study Genesis 1, it is therefore most fitting for us to ask this question about its first verse, Genesis 1:1: "In the beginning, God created the heavens and the earth."

God Transcendent

When we begin thinking about God, our first thought should concern the infinite distance between the Creator and the creation. We refer to this as the *transcendence* of God. People sometimes refer to God as the *Supreme Being*, which he certainly is. Compared to all other beings of every kind, God is supremely and infinitely above them all.

God is transcendent over everything else in terms of his nature. The Song of Moses asked, "Who is like you, O Lord

...? Who is like you, majestic in holiness, awesome in glorious deeds, doing wonders?" (Exodus 15:11). The point is that there is nothing to which we may suitably compare God, and for this reason theology often relies on negative statements. Unable to declare adequately what God *is*, we resort to stating what he *is not*: God is infinite, not finite; independent, not dependent; immutable, not capable of change. The reason for this transcendence of nature is evident in Genesis 1:1, "In the beginning, God." God existed prior to and wholly apart from his creation, so therefore nothing in the creation can encompass who and what he is.

God is not only transcendent in nature but also in time. Genesis 1:1 declares that in the beginning God already was, which presents him as an *eternal* being. Peter Lewis writes:

> Before there was matter, time and space there was God: God who has no succession of moments in his own Being, God who alone is infinite and eternal, the uncreated Creator, unique in his eternity and all-sufficient in the infinite resources of his Being, the fullness of light, love, joy and meaning: 'From everlasting to everlasting you are God' (Psalm 90:2).[14]

Contemplating such a God, believers find awe in worship and comfort in faith. Thus it was that Abraham, in the midst of his otherwise perplexing journeys, "called ... on the name of the LORD, the Everlasting God" (Genesis 21:33).

God Imminent and Personal

Genesis 1:1 not only pulls our thoughts infinitely upwards in contemplating God's transcendence, but also draws our hearts near to a personal God who is *imminent*. The very fact that "in the beginning, God created," indicates that he wills to be known and possess a relationship with beings outside of himself. The reason for this is that God is *personal* as well as transcendent. Being personal, God is known not merely in terms of impersonal characteristics, the way an object is measured, but in personal attributes.

Atheistic thinkers labor to support the idea of an impersonal original for all things, such as the Big Bang Theory. The reason for this quest is that a personal Creator implies that there is a divine will and purpose. We relate to the God of the Bible on personal terms, and since he is our Creator this requires worship, submission, and obedience—the very things our rebellious world desires to avoid. Paul perfectly diagnosed this situation in Romans 1:21, "For although they knew God, they did not honor him as God or give thanks to him." A personal God is honored and thanked for the great and good things he has provided, and this precludes us from acting as our own gods. Denying God's personal existence, Paul says men "became futile in their thinking, and their foolish hearts were darkened" (Romans 1:21).

The very fact of *creation* indicates a *personal* Creator, with will and intelligence. God is not a mere force, with matter mindlessly emanating from his being. This truth is powerfully shown by scientists involved in what is called "Intelligent Design" theory. They point out that nature involves complex creations, such as the human eye, that show an unquestioned design that could not be random products of evolution. In making this point, Intelligent Design theorists today are echoing the reasoning of ancient Greek philosophers such as Socrates and Plato, as well as the medieval scholars who laid the foundations of modern science. Isaac Newton, for instance, stated: "This most elegant system of the sun, planets, and comets could not have arisen without the design and dominion of an intelligent and powerful being."[15] Likewise, Genesis 1 shows God acting in a conscious manner according to a careful plan.

Since the impersonal cannot convey personhood, the greatest proof of God's personal nature is our own self-awareness. We have thoughts, feelings, and will. All of these are possible only because they are also true of the Creator. Denying this reality depersonalizes not only God but also ourselves. Francis Schaeffer notes: "The assumption of a impersonal beginning cannot adequately explain the personal beings we see around us; and when men try to explain man on the basis of an original impersonal, man soon disappears."[16]

In reality, since we are personal in our very nature, our deepest needs and longings can only be met by knowing the personal God who made all things. It is only a relational God who can guide us in pursuing loving human relationships, building just societies, and flowering a culture of beauty and dignity.

The Bible teaches that God exists in a unique form of personhood known as *Trinity*: a single divine being who exists eternally in a perfect, harmonious community of persons, the Father, Son, and Holy Spirit. This means that within God himself are things like love, fellowship, acceptance, and communication. These things happen to be the key to our own fulfillment as persons. God made mankind for relationships not only with one another but with himself.

It is as Trinity that God fulfills this purpose. God the Father made us with his own hands for a face-to-face personal relationship: "the LORD God formed the man of dust from the ground and breathed into his nostrils the breath of life" (Genesis 2:7). God the Son, the Second Person of the Trinity, Jesus Christ, became incarnate so we might see what God is like. "Whoever has seen me has seen the Father", Jesus said (John 14:9). It is then because of the Holy Spirit's indwelling presence that "man became a living creature" (Genesis 2:7) and that we may be illuminated inwardly for spiritual communion with God. Putting together the contributions of the entire Trinity, Paul speaks of the personal relationship into which we are called through faith in the triune God of the Bible: "For God, who said, 'Let light shine out of darkness,' has shone in our hearts to give the light of the knowledge of the glory of God in the face of Jesus Christ" (2 Corinthians 4:6).

If you are reading this, you are God's created person. He desires that you would enter into a personal, saving relationship with him through his Incarnate Son, by the power of his Holy Spirit, so that through faith the Creator would become your Father in heaven.

God Almighty

A third characteristic of the God revealed in Genesis 1:1 is seen in his ability to create all things out of nothing. God is, therefore, *omnipotent*. He is the Lord *Almighty*. These words mean that God possesses infinite power to do whatever he pleases. As the creation story unfolds, we find God's power glorified in both the difficulty and scale of what he accomplishes and in the ease with which he does it, by means of his mere word. The psalmist marvels: "By the word of the LORD the heavens were made, and by the breath of his mouth all their host ... For he spoke, and it came to be; he commanded, and it stood firm" (Psalm 33:6, 9).

God's power, like himself, is *infinite*. There is literally nothing that he desires that he cannot do. This omnipotence is necessary to his divine nature. A. W. Pink writes: "He who cannot do what he will and perform all his pleasure cannot be God. As God hath a will to resolve what He deems good, so has He power to execute his will."[17]

Christians totally rely on the infinite power of God to fulfill all that he has promised and achieve everything according to his Word. In fact, without God's infinite power, none of his other attributes could succeed in expression. Stephen Charnock writes:

> How vain would be the eternal counsels, if power did not step in to execute them. Without power His mercy would be but feeble pity, His promises an empty sound, His threatenings a mere scarecrow. God's power is like Himself: infinite, eternal, incomprehensible: it can neither be checked, restrained, nor frustrated by the creature.[18]

No wonder, then, that Christians praise God especially for his power. We noted earlier how Israel praised God's transcendence in the Song of Moses, after they passed through the Red Sea waters. They also praised God's power: "The LORD is my strength and my song, and he has become my salvation ... Your right hand, O LORD, glorious in power, your right hand, O Lᴏʀᴅ, shatters the enemy" (Exodus 15:2, 6).

God's power is not only infinite, but *sovereign*. This means that God's eternal will, empowered by his infinite might, is the ultimate cause and reason for everything. People sometimes recoil against the idea of God being in control of all things. But consider the God of Genesis 1:1, who made everything according to his own will and infinite power. A. W. Tozer writes: "Sovereignty and omnipotence must go together. One cannot exist without the other. To reign, God must have power, and to reign sovereignly, He must have all power. And that is what *omnipotent* means, having all power."[19] In fact, Genesis 1:1 provides one of the strongest declarations of God's absolute sovereignty: "In the beginning, God created the heavens and the earth."

God's manner of wielding power is *creative*. God's will does not have the aim of destruction, but rather God builds up and creates in marvelous wonder. In his creative wisdom, God has power not only to move great objects but to design and fashion stars, planets, puppies, flowers, and waterfalls. Out of his creative personality, God had power to create the spark of romance between a boy and girl, the surge of nobility within the human heart, and the compassionate desire to sacrifice for others in need. These are all creations of God. In coming to know God better and in glorifying him, it is therefore only natural for Christians to be lively and creative people who use God's gifts in line with the precepts he has given. William Still writes: "A Christian ought never to be dull nor the Christian life ever drab."[20] Christians honor God by employing the powerful creative gifts that he has given, through scientific study, artistic expression, and the exploration of the human condition through literature.

Finally, the Bible goes on to show that God's power is *redemptive*. God glorifies his power in the highest extent not in the raw scope of creation and its creative genius but in his saving power to overthrow sin in the lives of those whom he would save. God's omnipotence declares him able to do all things according to his will. But what if God's will is to love and restore rebellious and guilty sinners to himself, while still honoring his perfect justice? Is God able to do that? The answer is that God's power to overcome sin is glorified in the marvel of redemption through Jesus Christ.

In an achievement that boggles our minds far more than the greatest and most distant galactic star cluster, God sent his Son to become man, in order to pay the penalty of our sins on the cross. Peter writes: "You have been ransomed … not with perishable things such as silver and gold, but with the precious blood of Christ" (1 Peter 1:18–19). God's saving power is seen in Paul's remarkable formula: "where sin increased, grace abounded all the more" (Romans 5:20). God has the power through the Holy Spirit to change the hardened heart (Ezekiel 36:26), giving life to the spirit that was dead in sin and unbelief, so that we believe and enter into eternal life. You will experience the power of the Creator in his highest work, *redemption*, if through his Spirit you believe his gospel message and gain the forgiveness of your sins through faith in Jesus Christ.

A God to be Adored and Praised

Already we have learned so much about God in just the

Bible's first verse! He is transcendent, personal, and almighty. Imagine how much we will learn about God if we keep reading!

Having met God on the doorstep of the biblical revelation in Genesis 1:1, how should his creatures respond to these things? Bruce Milne writes: "Clearly they call for a deep self-abasement of ourselves before his awesome majesty, and highlight our obligation to offer him an adoring, submissive worship. Truly, 'Great is the Lord and most worthy of praise' (Psalm 96:4)."[21] In one of our beloved hymns, Christians sing praise to God for his creation:

> O Lord my God, when I in awesome wonder
>   consider all the worlds thy hands have made,
> I see the stars, I hear the rolling thunder,
>   thy power thro' out the universe displayed.
> Then sings my soul, my Savior God, to thee:
> How great thou art, how great thou art.[22]

When we get to the end of the Bible, we find that this impulse to worship God as Creator is fulfilled by the heavenly beings in glory: "Worthy are you, our Lord and God, to receive glory and honor and power, for you created all things, and by your will they existed and were created" (Revelation 4:11). This makes the point that our calling to worship God is grounded in the fact of God as our Creator. For while Christians have *abundant* reasons to praise God for our redemption, everyone has *every* reason to glorify God as our Maker. A. W. Pink exclaims: "The wondrous and infinite perfections of such a Being call for fervent worship. If men of might and renown claim the admiration of the world, how much more should the power of the Almighty fill us with wonderment and homage."[23]

Just as the Bible concludes with praise to God, our Creator and Redeemer, so also will history consummate in worship:

> When Christ shall come with shout of acclamation
>   and take me home, what joy shall fill my heart!
> Then I shall bow in humble adoration, and there proclaim,
>   my God, how great thou art.
> Then sings my soul, my Savior God, to thee:
> How great thou art, how great thou art.[24]

3   *God the Self-Existing*

Genesis 1:1

In the beginning, God created the heavens and the earth
(Genesis 1:1).

WHAT'S IN A NAME? IN OUR CULTURE, THE ANSWER IS OFTEN "not very much," as names are commonly given simply because of the way they sound. But in the Bible there is very much to a name. Moses knew this. Therefore as he received his commission to deliver Israel out of Egypt, he asked God: "If I come to the people of Israel and say to them, 'The God of your fathers has sent me to you,' and they ask me, 'What is his name?' what shall I say to them?" (Exodus 3:13). The answer was of the greatest significance. "God said to Moses, 'I Am Who I Am.' And he said, 'Say this to the people of Israel, "I Am has sent me to you"'" (Exodus 3:14). John Calvin wrote of this: "God attributes to himself alone divine glory, because he is self-existent and therefore eternal; and thus gives being and existence to every creature."[25] In this divine sense, only God can name himself, "I Am."

We have studied Genesis 1:1 being careful to learn what it tells us about the great God who is the subject of the Bible. In the previous chapter, we considered God's transcendence, personality, and omnipotence. Two of these—

transcendence and omnipotence—are what theologians refer to as incommunicable attributes of God. This means they are characteristics that are unique to the Godhead and cannot be communicated to his creatures. Before we depart from the Bible's first verse, we should consider other attributes revealed here that are essential to deity and vital to a right understanding of God.

We remember that when Moses began writing Genesis, he had already met God at the burning bush. Moses had been tending the flocks of his father-in-law Jethro when he saw a bush that "was burning, yet it was not consumed" (Exodus 3:2). There are no analogies for the being of God in nature, so God presented a supernatural analogy in the bush that burned but was not burned up. Just like the God who in the beginning created the heavens and the earth, the blazing fire did not have an evident source and was not dependent on created materials. God's nature, likewise, is self-existing and self-sufficient. And just as God told Moses to approach with reverence, taking the sandals off his feet, we also should appreciate that the study of God's divine attributes is holy ground.

The Self-Existence of God

As you get older, you sometimes receive birthday cards that note the often-forgotten events of your now distant birth year. I was born in 1960, which saw numerous events that have likely impacted your life. The first Roman Catholic, John F. Kennedy, was elected as President of the United States after the first televised presidential debates. Dr. Seuss published *Green Eggs and Ham* and Harper Lee's *To Kill a Mockingbird* rocked the literary world. On television, both *Rawhide* and *The Flintstones* first aired, while the movies *Ben Hur* and *Psycho* were released. An American spy plane was shot down over Russia, escalating Cold War tensions, and the Communist regime in Hanoi attacked South Vietnam, prompting the United States to send troops into that conflict.

If you were not alive when these events took place, then at that time you did not exist. There was a time when you were not, and then there was a time when you were, a date you recall as your birthday. Imagine, however, a being who does not have a birthday. There is no card that can be sent to him outlining the events of his first year. There was no time when he was not. There was no moment when he became. This being is God. God did not come into existence, because he has always existed. As Moses said, "From everlasting to everlasting, you are God" (Psalm 90:2).

Little children often begin their journey in theology by asking the question, "Mommy, who made the world?" She likely answers, "Why, God made the world." This only prompts a second question: "Then who made God?" The answer is one of the most important things we can know: "No one made God. God has always existed." This is one of the most vital attributes of God, known as his *aseity*. The Latin *a* means *from*, and *se* means *self*. God is from himself; he is self-existing.[26]

This statement does not mean that God created himself. It is a logical absurdity for something that did not exist to cause itself to exist. Rather, aseity means that God exists eternally in and of himself. Herman Bavinck writes: "All that God is, he is of himself."[27] God has always existed and his existence does not arise from anything or anyone else. This is one of the great differences between you and God. You have parents. However mysterious the origin of life always is, there still were biological events that resulted in your being. But no such things can be said about God. James Henley Thornwell writes: "He leans upon nothing. He lives no borrowed life. He asks no leave to be. He is because He is."[28] This is precisely what is in the name that God gave to Moses: "I Am That I Am."

The self-existence of God is a logical necessity to explain the existence of everything else. This point is known as the *cosmological argument* for God. Since it is an absurdity to believe that you can start with nothing and end with something, there must be a being who possesses self-existence. Since something which once did not exist could not have caused itself to exist, there must be a being which is uncaused and is thus the cause of all else. This is a question that Christians should ask atheists or agnostics, the latter being those who claim that we cannot know if there is a God. If there is not necessarily a God—a being with self-existence—then where logically did existence come from? R. C. Sproul states the case:

> If something exists, then something somewhere, somehow has to have the power of being within it, or nothing would be ... Why is there something rather than nothing? What or where is self-existent reality? The Scriptures answer that question on the very first page of the Old Testament: "In the beginning, God created the heavens and the earth." The first affirmation of Christianity is that God is the Creator. That God alone is eternal. That God alone has *aseity*. God alone has

self-existence. God alone has the power of being within himself. The difference between the human being and the Supreme Being is *being* rather than non-being.[29]

Christians admit that self-existence is beyond our ability to comprehend. But it is not illogical. Meanwhile, the atheist argument that there was existence without a cause is inherently irrational. And while philosophical arguments like this can never take the place of Scripture in proving Christianity, they can display the unreasonableness of atheistic unbelief. Difficult as self-existence is to understand, the implication of denying a self-existent God is logically irrational.

In Romans 1:20, Paul taught that God reveals his divine attributes to everyone by means of creation:

> For his invisible attributes, namely, his eternal power and divine nature, have been clearly perceived ever since the creation of the world, in the things that have been made.

The correct response, then, to the revelation of the self-existent God is to bow down and worship him. Those who suppress the awareness of God and refuse to worship him "are without excuse" (Romans 1:20).

The Self-Sufficiency of God

When we contemplate the Bible's first sentence, "In the beginning, God created the heavens and the earth," we must realize not only his self-existence but also the important matter of God's *self-sufficiency*. This means, since all things originate from God, that God has all things in himself and therefore has no need for anything outside of himself.

Thornwell explains: "It means that God contains within Himself the fullness of perfection and blessedness—that nothing can be taken from Him and nothing added to Him."[30] The *Westminster Confession* expresses this truth in classic terms:

> God hath all life, glory, goodness, blessedness, in and of himself; and is alone in and unto himself all-sufficient, not standing in need of any creatures which he hath made, nor deriving any glory from them ... He is the alone fountain of all being, of whom, through whom, and to whom are all things.[31]

This teaching may be hard to understand until we remember that all things originate from God, so that God possesses all things in himself. The burning bush, illustrating God's self-existence, also symbolizes his self-sufficiency: the fire did not depend on the bush for its fuel but burned by its own resources. Since God's perfect sufficiency does not depend on anything that happens in his creation, there is nothing in all the universe that can add to his blessing or subtract from his fullness.

People will counter that the very fact that God created the heavens and the earth shows that God desires the things he has made. This is of course true, but not because God lacks anything in himself that he is seeking through matter, history, or us. Rather, God simply desired to manifest the perfections of his glorious attributes through creation and then through redemption. Yet this desire for glory does not arise from a need, as if God did not eternally possess infinite glory. Jesus said, "the Father has life in himself" (John 5:26). Therefore, all that God needs he already possesses eternally.

Understanding God's self-sufficiency is important simply because our worship calls for a right and true understanding of God. There are, however, at least three practical implications. The first is that *God does not need our help*. We are never helping God meet his needs even as he helps us meet ours. Tozer writes: "We commonly represent Him as a busy, eager, somewhat frustrated Father hurrying about seeking help to carry out His benevolent plan to bring peace and salvation to the world."[32] Paul refuted this way of thinking in the great doxology of Romans 11:

> For who has known the mind of the Lord, or who has been his counselor? Or who has given a gift to him that he might be repaid? For from him and through him and to him are all things. To him be glory forever. Amen (Romans 11:34–36).

The God who made all things out of his own eternal resources does not need our help but yet graciously invites us to participate in his glorious work in history. God does not need our witness to convert the lost, but he welcomes us to play a major role in the salvation of others. So rather than being paralyzed by God's self-sufficiency, Christians will be emboldened by the certainty of his will and humbly motivated because he graciously invites us into his labor. God likewise told Moses, "I Am Who I Am," so that Moses would know that the resources of a self-existent and self-sufficient God were available to him as he acted boldly in obedience and faith. The same is true for us in serving the gospel today.

A second implication of divine self-sufficiency is that since God possesses in himself an infinite fullness of blessing, *the greatest aim of every creature is to possess God through saving faith.*

God is himself our greatest end, treasure, resource, and hope. Thornwell writes: "Poor in ourselves, without strength, without resources, feeble as a reed, and easily crushed before the moth, we are yet rich and valiant and mighty in God. We have treasures which can never be consumed, resources which can never be exhausted, and strength which can never fail."[33]

Third, the knowledge of God's self-sufficiency *should humble us so that we often pray with a true sense of our need*. How great is our need of the blessings that only God can provide out of his infinite fullness! Our endurance fails, so we should call on him who upholds all things with his own power. Isaiah rejoiced:

> The LORD is the everlasting God, the Creator of the ends of the earth. He does not faint or grow weary; his understanding is unsearchable. He gives power to the faint, and to him who has not might he increases strength ... they who wait for the LORD shall renew their strength (Isaiah 40:28–31).

The Immutability of God

There is one last attribute of God which we should consider here on the doorstep of biblical revelation, gazing on the God who in the beginning created the heavens and the earth. This is the attribute known as God's *immutability*. God, being self-existent and self-sufficient, does not and cannot change. For us, life involves constant flux, often for the worse. This is why fewer and fewer people connect with the events that took place in 1960, the year I was born, because it is increasingly long ago and things have changed so much since. But God is an eternal being, so that he does not and cannot change. He is immutable.

One reason that God does not change is that change implies a succession of events, whereas God dwells in an eternal present in which there is no succession. That is why he named himself, "I Am Who I Am" (Exodus 3:14). We are, in contrast, contingent beings who experience time as a succession of events. Our lives are like a boat that careens down a rapid-filled river, one harrowing twist after another. But God is the absolute being who looks down on the entirety of history all at once. God sees the entire river of history, knowing what for us is past and future all at the same time.

Divine immutability means that God never changes in his *being*. God always has been and always will be precisely as he is now. The *attributes* of God revealed in the Bible, including his holiness, truth, goodness, justice and love, will never alter. This means that while every human source of trust is bound eventually to fail, God himself will never fail. A. W. Pink writes:

> God has neither evolved, grown, nor improved. All that He is today, He has ever been, and ever will be … He cannot change for He is already perfect; and being perfect, He cannot change for the worse. Altogether unaffected by anything outside Himself, improvement or deterioration is impossible. He is perpetually the same. He only can say, "I am that I am" (Exodus 3:14).[34]

God further never changes in his *will* and *purpose*. Numbers 23:19 declares: "God is not man, that he should lie, or a son of man, that he should change his mind. Has he said, and will he not do it? Or has he spoken, and will he not fulfill it?" In

God's will, James says, "there is no variation or shadow due to change" (James 1:17).

People object and say that the Bible itself shows God's attitude and actions changing with respect to people. But it is not God and his will that have changed; it is the people who have changed through faith or unbelief. Philip Ryken comments: "The fact that God is immutable does not mean that he is immobile. Although his attributes do not change, God is active in possessing and exercising them. He always acts in a way that is consistent with himself."[35] Therefore amidst all the turbulent changes of life and history, God's will is perfectly fulfilled as it has been from all eternity. He declares: "I am God, and there is no other;... saying, 'My counsel shall stand and I will accomplish all my purpose'" (Isaiah 46:9–10).

The immutability of God, like his self-existence and self-sufficiency, is full of comfort for the believer in Christ. Thornwell writes, "The immutability of God is the foundation of all our hopes. It is here that the heirs of the promise have strong consolation. He can never deceive us in the expectations which He excites. He never falls short of, but often goes immeasurably beyond, what He had led us to expect. Here is the pledge of His faithfulness—He can never change; His counsel shall stand, and He will do all His pleasure."[36]

At the same time, God's unchangeableness is the great terror of the unbelieving and rebellious. It means that the dire threats of God's impending judgment will come true. Wilhelmus à Brakel therefore pleads for all who hear the gospel of Jesus Christ to repent and believe: "Since God is immutable, how you should fear, unconverted sinner! For all the threatenings and judgments, both temporal and eternal, with which you have been threatened, will certainly and unavoidably come upon you if you do not repent."[37]

The Great "I Am"

In his great chapter on faith, the writer of Hebrews began by noting that Christian belief starts at Genesis 1:1: "By faith we understand that the universe was created by the word of God, so that what is seen was not made out of things that are visible" (Hebrews 11:3). Having understood that God exists and that all things are from him, faith "must believe that he exists and that he rewards those who seek him" (Hebrews 11:6). The great issue of life, therefore, is to believe in God and seek a relationship with him. We look up at the stars, so vast and far away—how can tiny specks like us meet and know our Creator?

The answer to this greatest of questions is given in the Bible, as it tells us that the Creator himself has stepped across the boundary between heaven and earth in the person of his Son, Jesus Christ. This is the great Christian declaration. When Moses stood before the burning bush and received the command to go redeem Israel from Egypt, could he ever have imagined that the great "I Am" would himself take up flesh in order to be the Redeemer who frees us from our sin?

It is precisely Jesus' claim that he is the "I Am" of the Old Testament, the God who in the beginning created the heavens and the earth. John's Gospel is famous for Jesus' great "I Am" statements. In them, he not only reveals his self-existent glory and his self-sufficient resources, but he offers them to everyone who receives him in humble faith. "I am the bread of life," he said. "Whoever comes to me shall not hunger, and whoever believes in me shall never thirst" (John 6:35). "I am the resurrection and the life. Whoever believes in me, though he die, yet shall he live" (John 11:25). "I am the way, the truth, and the life," Jesus declared. "No one comes to the Father except through me" (John 14:6). By taking up this great name, "I Am," Jesus declared his own nature as the God who in the beginning created the heavens and the earth, the God who possesses all life and sufficiency in himself. He is sufficient even to remove the guilt of your sin, saying, "I am the good shepherd. The good shepherd lays down his life for the sheep" (John 10:11).

Since Jesus is the self-existent, self-sufficient God, then like the Father he is also immutable. Hebrews 13:8 says: "Jesus Christ is the same yesterday and today and forever." Therefore, Jesus will treat you just as he did the needy sinners in the Bible. If you seek him, as they did, you will find your meaning in the self-existent God and gain your fulfillment in the self-sufficient Creator. And when you receive the forgiveness of your sins at the cross of Jesus you will know that your acceptance into the love of God will never change.

4   *The Architecture of Creation*

Genesis 1:1–2

The earth was without form and void, and darkness was upon the face of the deep. And the Spirit of God was hovering over the face of the waters (Genesis 1:2).

IN 415 BC, THE ATHENIAN NAVY DESCENDED ON THE ISLAND OF Sicily with an invading army. For over a year, Athens besieged the fortress city of Syracuse, blockading its port and constructing a wall to cut off the city from support. This siege was one of the most decisive events of the ancient world, since victory would have opened the way for an Athenian conquest of Italy and removed Rome from future world affairs. By 414 BC, the people of Syracuse were so disheartened that they called an assembly to discuss the terms of surrender they might offer to Athens. At this critical moment, however, a small ship was seen evading the blockading squadron and headed towards the harbor. The deliberation stopped as the citizens watched the ship draw near. When it arrived, a messenger from Athens' chief rival, Sparta, emerged in the assembly with news that help was on the way in the form of the Spartan general Gylippus. Their drooping spirits energized, the Syracusans resolved to continue fighting and with Sparta's help they went on to defeat the Athenian invaders.[38]

It is not hard to discern the hand of God in these events, especially as they shaped the future of the world into which Jesus would come and in which the gospel would be spread. Moreover, the pattern seen in this scenario is typical of God's working in history. What was needed was an infusion of spiritual energy so that faith would be uplifted. This pattern, so often seen in world history, is even more prominent in redemption, where the Holy Spirit provides the spiritual power necessary to saving faith. So significant is this pattern of spiritual energizing that its presence is seen even in the opening phase of God's work of creation. Moses writes that in the primeval state of creation, when all was a deep and dark mass, "the Spirit of God was hovering over the face of the waters" (Genesis 1:2). The result was life and energy for God's creation design.

Relating Genesis 1:1 and 1:2

As we move from the Bible's first verse toward the narrative that follows, there are a couple of questions that demand our attention. The first question concerns whether Genesis 1:1 records an actual event or serves merely as a sort of chapter heading, the way a good academic paper today begins with a clear thesis statement. The significance of this question is that if Genesis 1:1 is only a title, saying something like, "This chapter is about how God created the universe," then it does not necessarily assert creation *ex nihilo*—creation out of nothing. If Genesis 1:1 does not record an actual historical event of the original creation, then the creation story starts in verse 3, where "God said, 'Let there be light,' and there was light." In this case, creation begins with the already existing matter that is mentioned in verse 2. Genesis 1 thus presents not true creation but the reforming of the chaotic matter already in the universe.

The great majority of conservative scholars insist that Genesis 1:1 teaches creation *ex nihilo*. John Calvin asserts that the verb used for "created" (Hebrew *bara*) implies original creation.[39] Moreover, while Genesis 1:1 does majestically introduce the chapter, there is no doubt that it serves as more than a title sentence. In its own terms, Genesis 1 reports the event of the original creation. Moreover, Hebrews 11:3 plainly states creation *ex nihilo* as the Bible's own interpretation of Genesis 1: "By faith we understand that the universe was created by the word of God, so that what is seen was not made out of things that are visible." C. John Collins writes: "Taking Genesis 1:1 as a background event, prior to the main storyline [which begins at verse 3], is the best way to read it ... The first verse of Genesis briefly records the creation of the universe in its essential form."[40]

A second question concerns how Genesis 1:1 and 1:2 relate to one another. In the early 1800s, Thomas Chalmers was a noted theologian and also an amateur geologist. At that time, evidence from rock formations was being used to argue for a much older age of the earth than is accounted for in the Bible. Wanting to harmonize Scripture and science, Chalmers proposed what is known as the "Gap Theory." This view argues that between Genesis 1:1 and 1:2 there is a large gap of time—perhaps millions of years—after which a cataclysm took place that made a ruin of God's original creation. Under this view, the expression, "The earth was without form and void," describes the result of God's judgment for the rebellion of Satan and his angels.[41] The original creation was thus made into a ruin which had to be repaired. This Gap Theory was included in the Dispensational notes to the influential Schofield Study Bible and in this way became a standard teaching among conservative Christians in the late nineteenth and early twentieth centuries.

There are a number of reasons, however, to rule out the Gap Theory. First, like the abyss it describes, the doctrine is created out of a void of biblical data. There is nothing in the text to suggest a massive time gap between verses 1 and 2, or to suppose that it assumes the rebellion of Satan. The grammar of Genesis 1:2 is even more conclusive in refuting the Gap Theory. The issue has to do with the Hebrew conjunction *waw*, signified by the letter *w*. When attached to the beginning of verbs, it notes a sequence of events and is translated "and." This would be the case if Genesis 1:2 was teaching something like the Gap Theory: first God created and then "the earth was without form and void." The problem is that verse 2 employs the *waw* not with a verb but a noun, in which case it is *disjunctive* rather than *consecutive*. The *waw disjunctive* does not note a sequence of events but rather interrupts a sequence to describe the situation. Thus Genesis 1:1–2 does not describe two different events separated by a massive gap in time and a cataclysmic rebellion against God. Rather, it records the initial creation and then gives three descriptions of the state of affairs that existed: "The earth was without form and void," "darkness was over the face of the deep," and "the Spirit of God was hovering over the face of the waters."

Formless and Void

We should not be surprised that an event as unique as the original creation is described in provocative and distinctive language. This is precisely the case with the first description of what the original creation was like before God began molding it: "The earth was without form and void" (Genesis 1:2).

This stark language has caused many to suggest that there was an initial chaos, a desolation and abyss to the original creation. The Hebrew words for "formless and void" are *tohu* and *bohu*, and they are found together in Isaiah 34:11 where God had punished Edom with "confusion" (*tohu*) and "emptiness" (*bohu*). Based on this and other biblical comparisons, H. C. Leupold translates them as "wilderness" and "emptiness."[42] Genesis 1:2 thus describes the original creation as barren and uninhabited: it was a desert and it was deserted.

Although these terms are later used to describe the effects of God's judgment, in Genesis 1:2 God is not destroying but creating. It thus describes a lack in the original creation, not because God has torn down but rather because he has not yet built it up. John Sailhamer writes that this formula "refers to the condition of the land in its 'not-yet' state—the state it was in before God made it 'good.'"[43] The raw material was there, but it had not yet been suitably fashioned. The situation was comparable to when Michelangelo received the great block of marble from which he would sculpt his famous statue of Israel's King David. Michelangelo gazed on the formless block, imagined the form of David inside it, and then set about the work of bringing forth what his genius had seen. Like Michelangelo, God looked into the primeval mass of creation and saw his intention to create a lush world filled with a blessed people.

The creation mass was not yet formed or inhabited, but this wonderful purpose was on the Creator's mind. God looks upon you, as well, with a sense of purpose and design for your blessing. Jeremiah 29:11 says, "I know the plans I have for you, declares the LORD, plans for welfare and not for evil, to give you a future and a hope."

This pair of terms, *tohu* and *bohu*, barren and uninhabited, sets up the progression that will be fulfilled in the six days of creation that follow. Days 1–3 serve to address the barren state of the creation: the day and night are separated, the land and the sea are distributed, and finally on the third day the earth is made to sprout with vegetation: "plants yielding seeds, and fruit trees bearing fruit in which is their seed" (Genesis 1:11). Days 4–6 then address the desertedness of the creation: lights are hung to guide the day and the night, sea creatures fill the waters, flying creatures soar in the air, and beasts creep on the ground. Finally, the pinnacle of God's creation took place on Day 6: "Then God said, 'Let us make man in our image, after our likeness'" (Genesis 1:26). God's plan for creation, then, involved the making of a home and a family.

This same pattern revealed in creation is repeated in God's work of redemption. Genesis 2 shows God creating a lush garden—a land—and placing his image-bearing man and woman into the garden to populate it with children—a people. The fall of man in sin caused the cursing of the land and the expulsion of the people. But starting in Genesis 12, God called Abraham to begin a work of salvation by grace. And notice what God offered Abraham—a promised land and people! "Go from your country and your kindred and your father's house to the land that I will show you. And I will make of you a great nation" (Genesis 12:1–2). Likewise, when Israel left their bondage in Egypt, they journeyed to the same promise: a promised land and a promised nation.

This means that Genesis 1:2 structures what God is doing through and for us today. When we come to Jesus in saving faith, God is providing us with an eternal home in which to dwell and a beloved people in which we have a part. Do you mean that God saw all of this—even his plans for me—when he looked on the "formless and void" mass of the original creation? Yes! In the mind of God was an architecture for creation that would flow into his work for our salvation. This is why the last chapter of the Bible so carefully mirrors the first chapter, Genesis 1. At the Bible's end we see the conclusion—still yet to appear in history—of God's purpose and plan in the beginning. Genesis 1:2 says, "The earth was *desolate* and *deserted*," and Revelation 22 answers with its vision of the eternal city in which flows "the river of the water of life" (Revelation 22:1) and the people "who wash their robes" and "have the right to the tree of life" (Revelation 22:14). God intended from the very beginning to make a glorious home for his beloved people. This is one way in which we see the gospel in the book of Genesis: it is in Christ that God ultimately achieves this aim, making us his holy people in order to live with him forever.

Darkness on the Deep

There is a second clause in Genesis 1:2 which relates another feature of the original creation: "and darkness was on the face of the deep" (Genesis 1:2). Here again, many scholars see an allusion to evil, some comparing this clause to the mythological creation stories of the ancient Near East, where the dragon Tiamat had to be wrestled and destroyed. But, again, there is no evidence of anything here other than what God desired. Science today shows that darkness is simply the absence of light, and likewise Genesis 1:3 shows that it was dark in the primeval mass simply because God had not yet shined his light upon it.

Particularly mysterious is "the face of the deep." It seems that this refers to the primeval mass which, as the verse goes on to say, consisted of "waters." From a scientific point of view, Andrew Kulikovsky suggests that "on the first day God created a three-dimensional space containing a ball of liquid water large enough to contain all the mass of the universe."[44] An alternative scenario sees the deep as "a massively deep layer of water covering or surrounding the surface of the barren and desolate earth."[45]

Again, the scenario of the original creation indicates a raw mass of potential on which God had not yet begun his work of fashioning and blessing. God did not intend for his creation to lie in darkness! So his first act after creation was to ordain light to shine on it: "And God said, 'Let there be light,' and there was light" (Genesis 1:3).

Bible readers inevitably look back on the earliest chapters of the Old Testament in light of the later teaching of the prophets. We remember, thus, the promise of Isaiah 9:2: "The people who walked in darkness have seen a great light; those who dwelt in a land of deep darkness, on them has light shined." It is God's will to bring light of every kind into places of darkness. Where there is ignorance, he provides truth. Where there is immorality, he cleanses for holiness. Reading further in the Bible, we find that Isaiah was looking forward to the Messiah, Jesus Christ. Christ was the light who would shine through his gospel on the people living in unbelief, ignorance, and sin. John 1:4 declares the ultimate remedy in the person of Jesus Christ: "In him was life and the life was the light of men."

The Spirit of God Hovering

The first two clauses of Genesis 1:2 identify problems in the original creation. They weren't defects but simply unfulfilled potential. In the final clause of Genesis 1:2, we see the beginning of the solution in the agent who will shine both life and light to the barren earth: "And the Spirit of God was hovering over the face of the waters."

There is, of course, scholarly debate about "the Spirit of God" in this verse, since the Hebrew might be taken as "the divine wind," a turbulent force stirring up the barren and chaotic mass. However, when the Hebrew word for "breath" (*rhuach*) is combined with "God" (*Elohim*), the meaning is always either God's Spirit or God's breath. In this case, the text describes personal actions rather than an impersonal influence: "the Spirit of God was hovering." Deuteronomy 32:11 uses the same verb to describe God as "an eagle that stirs up its nest, that flutters over its young." A mother eagle hovers over her nest, stirring up her hatchlings to growth and vitality. In the same manner, the Spirit of God fluttered over the waters of the original creation, ready to provide the power and life that would bring the Father's purpose to fulfillment. With what anticipation Genesis 1:2 ends! The Spirit of God was awaiting the mighty Word of God, by which life and light would shine upon the world of God's creation!

The Spirit Who Makes All the Difference

When the Spartan general Gylippus arrived in Syracuse, his mere presence made all the difference. Though bringing no troops or war materials, he lifted their spirits with an infusion of confidence, wisdom, and will. History records this as just one of many episodes in which the difference was made by the infusion of a new spirit, with power and vigor.

This incident illustrates the blessing presented in Genesis 1:2 by the hovering presence of the greatest of all spirits, the Holy Spirit of the living God. The verse begins shrouded in all that was lacking: a barren, deserted, and dark mass. Reading the first two statements it seems hard to see how such a condition could lead to something so glorious and great. But what a difference the Spirit makes! By the mighty Spirit of God, the creation would soon pulse with order, power, blessing, and life.

The same condition prevails in the lives of men and women. How many people, communities, even entire cultures can be described with the ominous terms of Genesis 1:2—desolate, empty, and dark. One cause is our own ruinous and sinful actions, making a desolation of our lives. Added to this is the just wrath of the holy God, so that our lives can seem a true *tohu* and *bohu*, with the darkness of evil and sin brooding on the face of our world. Perhaps you can connect with this kind of situation. Is your life chaotic? Disordered? Empty and vain? Broken and dark? If so, you may feel that all is without hope.

But read Genesis 1:2 and remember what a difference the
Spirit of God will make! We have hope in the very Spirit of
God who hovered over the primeval dark of the first creation
and is still fluttering over this world. God's Spirit is ready to
act in the cause of the Savior whose gospel offers salvation
to all who will believe. R. Kent Hughes writes: "Just as the
Spirit of God fluttered over the dark waters, so he does over
the dark hearts of humanity, preparing them for the word of
God that will make them into new creations in Christ."⁴⁶

Does this mean that I can be made new, just like the first
creation? Is it possible that I can be a new person, bearing the
life and light of God? The Bible's answer is Yes! If you ask the
Father in Jesus' name to send the Spirit into your life, Jesus
promises that he will. After all, earthly fathers give blessings to
their children. So Jesus promises, "how much more will the
heavenly Father give the Holy Spirit to those who ask him!"
(Luke 11:13). Maybe you are not yet a believer. Then ask God
in Jesus' name to send the Spirit and his life-transforming
power! Perhaps you have long trusted in the Lord. You too
should pray for the Spirit's invigorating work. God's Spirit
comes into our lives as we receive God's Word in faith. As
Paul wrote: "our gospel came to you not only in word, but
also in power and in the Holy Spirit and with full conviction"
(1 Thessalonians 1:5).

How can I know that God's Spirit is working in me with
saving power? Here, we may see an analogy in the sequence
of events in Genesis 1:2 and 1:3. First, the Spirit of God was
hovering over the face of the deep. What was he waiting
for? He was waiting for the Word of God to shine light into
darkness. Indeed, if the Spirit is fluttering over your barren

soul, you can be sure that he is seeking for you to believe
the message of the Bible that will truly change your life:
"For God so loved the world, that he gave his only Son, that
whoever believes in him should not perish but have eternal
life" (John 3:16).

5   *Fiat Lux!*

Genesis 1:3–5

And God said, "Let there be light," and there was light. And God saw that the light was good. And God separated the light from the darkness (Genesis 1:3–4).

YOU MIGHT HAVE NOTICED THAT AS CHRISTIANS WE ARE studying Genesis 1 in light of the New Testament. We should be doing this, because the Bible is one unified message with God as its author. And yet someone would be right to warn, "Not so fast!" While reading a passage in light of the whole Bible, we also need to consider it carefully in its own original context and setting. The Bible says that Moses wrote Genesis during the redemption of Israel from bondage in Egypt. Exodus 24:4 tells us that Moses actually began writing while still atop Mount Sinai, in the presence of God. Later, he would go into the tabernacle "to speak with the LORD" (Numbers 7:89).

This means that the original readers of Genesis (or, more likely, hearers), were ancient Israel, a pilgrim people sojourning through the wilderness towards the Promised Land. We need to remember this exodus context, even as we study Genesis from a Christian perspective. The Israelites walked at night under the bright canopy of lights shining down from above. Inside the tabernacle, the dark spaces were lit by candles on the seven-stemmed lampstand. Through God's Word, Moses told them that the very God who made the light to shine above was shining the gospel in their hearts. The God who said, "'Let there be light,' and there was light," was the Lord whose Word they trusted in seeking their home far away.

The Word in the Beginning

So far in our study, we have noticed the presence of two of the members of the Trinity. It was God the Father who "in the beginning ... created the heavens and earth" (Genesis 1:1). Then we saw God the Spirit "hovering over the face of the waters" (Genesis 1:2). As Christians, we should suspect the presence of God the Son as well. After all, Paul wrote that by Jesus "all things were created, in heaven and on earth ... all things were created through him and for him" (Colossians 1:16). Hebrews 1:2 identifies Christ as "the heir of all things, through whom [God] also created the world." If all things were created by and through God the Son, we would expect to see him in Genesis 1. Where, then, is Christ in the creation?

The answer is seen in Genesis 1:3: "And God said, 'Let there be light,' and there was light." The Gospel of John explains how this relates to Christ by referring to Jesus as the divine Word: "In the beginning was the Word, and the Word was with God, and the Word was God. He was in the beginning with God. All things were made through him, and without him was not any thing made that was made" (John 1:1–3). The deliberate link to the opening lines of Genesis is obvious.

The New Testament depicts Christ's salvation as a new work of creation, so it is no surprise that it also places Jesus as God and with God in creating the heavens and earth.

John 1:1 teaches Jesus' deity in terms of his eternal and divine personhood. Genesis 1:3 shows that God created by means of the Word, so that the Word—Christ—existed prior to creation. Just as Genesis 1:1 says, "In the beginning, God," John 1:1 declares: "In the beginning was the Word." When the creation "was made," Jesus already "was"! This was an important statement in the church's fight with Arius, whose denial of Christ's deity prompted the Council of Nicaea in 325 AD. Arius maintained that while Jesus was god-like in many ways, he was still a created being and less than fully God. But John 1:1 and Genesis 1:3 tell us that when time and creation began, Jesus already "was." Leon Morris says, "The Word existed before creation, which makes it clear that the Word … is not to be included among created beings."[47]

By connecting Jesus to Genesis 1:3, John wants us to understand not only the eternity of the Word but also his personhood. The Word is a person, the companion of God himself! This warns us against another perennial heresy, that which denies the distinct personhood of the various members of the Trinity. The doctrine of the Trinity states, "In the unity of the Godhead there are three persons … God the Father, God the Son, and God the Holy Spirit."[48] When John identifies Jesus as the Word of Genesis 1:3, he means God the Son, Jesus Christ, who eternally lives in relationship with and does the will of God the Father. The Word is God's executor in creation, the servant who accomplishes God's will. Jesus prayed likewise to the Father at the end of his earthly ministry: "I glorified you on earth, having accomplished the work that you gave me to do" (John 17:4).

Seeing Jesus' glorious presence in the opening moments of creation helps us to appreciate his humility in coming to die for our sins. As Paul pointed out, Jesus "emptied himself, by taking the form of a servant, being born in the likeness of men. And being found in human form, he humbled himself by becoming obedient to the point of death, even death on a cross" (Philippians 2:7–8). Sidney Greidanus writes: "The King of the universe became a slave. When the world was headed for destruction, God spoke his word again through Jesus ... The Word of God, Jesus, created this world, and the Word of God, Jesus, will redeem this world."[49] This holy thought informs one of our beloved Christmas carols:

> Come to earth to taste our sadness,
>   he whose glories knew no end;
> By his life he brings us gladness,
>   our Redeemer, Shepherd, Friend.
> Leaving riches without number,
>   born within a cattle stall;
> This the everlasting wonder,
>   Christ was born the Lord of all.[50]

And God Said

Our Christian understanding of Genesis 1:3 would not have been as apparent to the original readers of Genesis. To them, the main point would have been the sheer power of God as he created by means of his mere word: "God said, 'Let there be light,' and there was light" (Genesis 1:3). As Psalm 33:6 would later extol: "By the word of the LORD the heavens were made, and by the breath of his mouth all their host."

It is highly significant that God's first action in creation was to speak: "And God said." We encounter this formula ten times in Genesis 1, so that "God said" forms the drumbeat of the marching creation. This reminds us, like verse 1, of the radical distinction between the Creator and his creation. Gerhard von Rad writes: "Creation cannot be even remotely considered an emanation from God; it is not somehow an overflow or reflection of his being ... but is rather a product of his personal will."[51] Moreover, "And God said" highlights how God's purpose is achieved and worked out by the going forth of his Word. Joining the presence of the Spirit in verse 2 to the creative Word in verse 3, starting the pattern that is repeated throughout Scripture: the activity of the Spirit joined to the ministry of God's Word. As the Spirit-blessed Word created light in the beginning, so also does the Spirit-blessed Word shine divine light into the hearts of sinners to create new life through faith in Jesus Christ.

The Latin version of Genesis 1:3 gives us the expression *creation by fiat.* "Fiat lux," says the Vulgate Bible: "Let there be light." By saying, "Let there be," God was expressing his will. Here, at the beginning of the Bible, we learn a lesson that will be vital for all of history and life: God's will is the creative and determining power of all that there is and will be. We ask the question if God is able to accomplish whatever he wills. The answer is that it was his will in the first place that created all things, causing even the first perfect rays of light to shine. God's will is a sovereign, creative power, enforced by his Word of command. Whatever God's Word declares to

be his will, whether it is a promise of salvation or a warning
of dire judgment, we may be absolutely certain that his will
will be done.

Notice, too, how God's will in creation shows his lordship
over all things. In contrast to the secular philosophy that sees
history as governed by chance events, Walter Brueggemann
writes: "The design of the world is not autonomous or
accidental. It is based upon the will of God ... The shape
of reality can only be understood as the purpose of God ...
Creation is what it is because God commands it."[52] The same
principle extends to each of us: we exist as we are because of
the will of God and we are designed to respond obediently to
God's will as it is revealed in his holy Word.

Genesis 1:3 especially displays the power by which God's
Word is always effectual: "And God said, 'Let there be light.'
And there was light." The Word of God possesses the power
of God to accomplish the will of God! Alasdair Paine observes
how much this tells us about God: "He is not silent; he may
be known, because he speaks. And look what happens when
he does: a universe springs into being."[53]

Christians should remember the power of God's Word
in creation when we are challenged to bear witness to the
Bible before an unbelieving world. How can we dare speak
unpalatable truths, convicting truths, truths that offend
the ears of idolatrous unbelievers, in the face of all manner
of secular and spiritual opposition? The answer is that we
know that God has willed the light of his Word to shine
and by means of that Word to grant new life so that sinners
will believe. Christians are, Peter said, "a royal priesthood,"
commissioned to "proclaim the excellencies of him who

called you out of darkness into his marvelous light" (1 Peter 2:9). Moreover, the same Word that powerfully created light and converted us as sinners goes on with that same power to cultivate God's sanctifying grace in our lives. This is why discerning believers have always given a priority to the Word of God in the witness and worship of the church and in the daily life of the faithful Christian.

Psalm 33 sets the pattern for how we should respond to the power of God exhibited through his Word in creation. First, it declares the fact: "For he spoke, and it came to be; he commanded, and it stood firm" (Psalm 33:9). Our response is given in the preceding verse: "Let all the earth fear the Lord; let all the inhabitants of the world stand in awe of him!" (Psalm 33:8). Indeed, the scenes of worship in the book of Revelation show that awe-inspired praise for the power of God in creation is the very theme of heaven. The heavenly beings cry out in wonder: "Worthy are you, our Lord and God, to receive glory and honor and power, for you created all things, and by your will they existed and were created" (Revelation 4:11).

And There Was Light

God spoke on the first day of creation and made light itself: "not just visible light, but the entire electromagnetic spectrum itself, apart from any light sources."[54] This is the Christian answer to those who scoff at the literal possibility of Genesis 1:3, since it presents light shining prior to the creation of the sun. But the sun is not the cause of light. God is the creator of light. Moreover, just as one would not create a musical instrument before sound itself had been made, it is entirely logical that God would make light on the first day before later making objects to shine and reflect that light.

In the Bible, just as in our earthly experience, light is associated with the flourishing of life. If you want a plant to grow, you place it in the sunshine. Light furthermore reveals. When you walk into a dark room, you turn on the light in order to see. It is not surprising then, that in revealing his glory through the work of creation, God began with the shining of light. Starting on the first day, creation would take place in the light of God's revelation. Light also speaks of safety and salvation. "The LORD is my light and my salvation," David wrote; "whom shall I fear?" (Psalm 27:1).

Given the numerous blessings associated with light, it is no wonder that verse 4 continues: "And God saw that the light was good." How wonderful that after speaking his very first creative word, on the first day of creation, God looks on what he has done and finds pleasure in it! We will be contemplating the goodness of creation all through Genesis 1, a truth that our damaged world needs help remembering. As Gordon Wenham writes: "God the great artist is pictured admiring his handiwork. This account of creation is a hymn to the Creator: creation itself bears witness to the greatness and goodness of God."[55]

God not only delighted in the light but he knew how beneficial it would be to his creatures. The light is a reflection of God's blessed nature. Psalm 18:28 extols: "the LORD my God lightens my darkness." The great Aaronic blessing made light synonymous with the expression of God's favor: "The LORD bless you and keep you; the LORD make his face to shine upon you and be gracious to you" (Numbers 6:24–25). God's approval signifies the perfection of his creation in fulfilling his will. We, too, should approve all that God does, learning to assign value in keeping with his measure of what is good and true. Therefore, whenever we see how beautiful is the light of God rising majestically above the morning horizon, we should praise our Maker, who shined light into darkness.

Think of what Genesis 1:3–4 would have meant to the people of Israel when they first heard these words from the lips of Moses. The dark nights of Sinai were cold and threatening, stirring fear and foreboding in their hearts. But light dawned on each new day, and as it shone they learned from Genesis that the God whose Word they were following was the very same God who created the light itself. God provided a special light, his *Shekinah Glory*, to shine on a difficult path as they trudged through a wilderness towards a land that God had promised. The light testified to the sovereign goodness of the Lord, urging them to go forward with confidence and expectation. Under the shining light that God had made, they could believe and keep his commands. David would later connect God's light to the guidance that comes to those who follow his Word: "Your word is a lamp to my feet and a light to my path" (Psalm 119:105).

The first day saw not only the first shining of light but also God's first act of division: "And God separated the light from the darkness" (Genesis 1:4). By separating, God provided one sphere for the light and another sphere for the darkness. Verse 5 elaborates: "God called the light Day, and the darkness he called Night. And there was evening and there was morning, the first day."

It is impossible to avoid the impression that darkness is

foreboding and evil. Certainly Scripture will often give this idea, just as every child instinctively struggles with fear of the dark. But we should hold off on such thoughts as we consider the first day. All that existed was made by God according to his perfect will. There is a place and role for darkness just as there is for day. God's division of light and darkness, day and night, provides a rhythm to life. There is a time for work and a time for rest. John Calvin preached:

> When lying down and rising up, we must bless his name for protecting us through the night and watching over us while we were asleep. And when day is at hand, let us also thank him for bringing us to a new life.[56]

In naming both the light and the darkness, God claims his sovereign rights as Creator: "God called the light Day, and the darkness he called Night" (Genesis 1:5). God is Lord over both, so that whatever fear we experience in facing them may be brought to him for our aid. Whatever purposes are pursued in them are ruled and judged by God, so that both day and night are to be spent in his service. In separating the light from the darkness, God gave order to the progression of time under his kingship. Psalm 19:2 offers them both to the praise of his revealed glory: "Day to day pours out speech, and night to night reveals knowledge."

The Light of the World

In the Jerusalem of Jesus' day, the Feast of Tabernacles was concluded each year with a festival of lights at the temple. Great candelabras were lit, casting beams throughout the city, to remember the guidance and protection that God gave in the exodus. It was probably in the midst of this illumination, six months before his death on the cross, that Jesus stood forth and proclaimed, "I am the light of the world" (John 8:12).

There are so many ways in which Jesus legitimately made this claim. He was, after all, the Word with whom the Father created light itself on the first day. As light was given to reveal, Jesus came to be the perfect image of God to mankind. He said: "Whoever has seen me has seen the Father" (John 14:9). Jesus is the light who provides salvation to men and women trapped in the darkness of sin. Isaiah foretold his coming in just these terms: "the people who walked in darkness have seen a great light; those who dwelt in a land of deep darkness, on them has light shined" (Isaiah 9:2). Jesus is the light of the world. Just as he was the source for the first light that shone through the darkness in creation, so also will he shine God's light on our paths. Therefore, he claims, "Whoever follows me will not walk in darkness, but will have the light of life" (John 8:12).

Reading the creation account, it is tempting to wonder what it would be like to have seen those brilliant first beams piercing the cosmic darkness. The marvel of the gospel is that we are not so distant from that light as some might think. On the first day, the Spirit of God was hovering as the Word of God said, "Let there be light," and there was light. The Spirit and the Word have not ceased in the work they began on that first day. By the Word of God, the Spirit is shining the light of God to give life, reveal truth, and bring salvation to everyone who believes. Paul said that just as Jesus was the source for the first light shining through the darkness in creation, he will also shine that very light into our hearts as we believe: "For God, who said, 'Let light shine out of darkness,' has shone in our

hearts to give the light of the knowledge of the glory of God
in the face of Jesus Christ" (2 Corinthians 4:6).

6   *The Days of Creation*

Genesis 1:5

God called the light Day, and the darkness he called Night.
And there was evening and there was morning, the first day
(Genesis 1:5).

THERE IS A TENDENCY IN THE STUDY OF GENESIS 1 FOR scholars to insist that we should not expect it to teach science but only theology. Saint Augustine is quoted in support, saying that in Genesis God "wanted to make Christians, not mathematicians."[57] The problem with this emphasis is noted by E. J. Young: "Inasmuch as the Bible is the Word of God, whenever it speaks on any subject, whatever that subject may be, it is accurate in what it says. The Bible may not have been given to teach science as such, but it does teach about the origin of all things."[58] This being the case, Herman Bavinck urges that when the Bible "speaks about the origin of heaven and earth … [it] deserves faith and trust. And for that reason, Christian theology, with but few exceptions, has held fast to the literal, historical view of the account of creation."[59]

Science and the Bible

As we proceed in our study of Genesis 1 from God's initial acts, we enter into the six days of creation, followed by the seventh day of rest. Before we go further, it is important for us to consider how we will read the material in the rest of the chapter. Since the main problem in the study of Genesis 1 lies in the conflict between its chronology and the findings of secular science, we should first arrive at some principles for relating the Bible to science.

God has revealed himself in two ways: through *general revelation*, that is, nature, and *special revelation*, the Holy Scriptures. In principle, we hold that they agree, having the same perfect author in God. With this in mind, Christians should be appreciative of science. Vern Poythress writes: "The Bible indicates that God created and governs all things. His wise and consistent governance is the basis for doing science. Science, rightly understood, endeavors to understand the mind of God and the wisdom of God in governing nature."[60]

The problems come when the findings of science and Scripture conflict. In approaching this problem, we need to consider science rightly. Secularists often speak of *objective* science. But the data of science always needs an interpreter, and the human interpreter is never objective, but approaches data with bias and preconceptions. They are, of course, also influenced by sin, which promotes a bias against the truth of God. Young writes: "We must remember that much that is presented as scientific fact is written from a standpoint that is hostile to supernatural Christianity."[61]

Another expression to reject is the declaration of *settled science*. Opponents of Christianity will often argue that evolution and other theories for our origin are settled beyond argument. But by its very nature science is never settled. At best, scientists work with a small amount of the overall potential data and must always be willing to consider new information. Mark Ross thus warns against the tendency to accommodate the Bible to science:

> Those who think that Biblical teaching must give way to scientific teaching whenever conflicts arise perhaps have not given adequate attention to the corrigibility of scientific findings. Today's accepted scientific "truth" might well turn out to be tomorrow's discarded theory.[62]

In contrast to science, the Bible is the revealed Word of God, and so has none of the limitations of human beings. God possesses all of the data, not merely a part, and was himself the actor in creation. Being holy in his perfect nature, God is always trustworthy. Therefore, while Christians should not flippantly discount the arguments of science, we should not place science in authority over God's Word. Poythress writes: "Since the Bible is infallible, we should give it the preference when conflicts between the Bible and science seem to arise."[63] If nature is a book for us to read, John Calvin points out that the inerrant Scriptures are the spectacles we wear in order to read it rightly.[64]

Of course, just as scientists are imperfect readers of nature, Christians are also imperfect readers of Scripture. We also possess biases and are prone to error. The most famous example is the medieval church's opposition to Galileo's heliocentric theory of the solar system. Roman Catholic authorities pointed to Joshua 10:12–13, where God caused the sun to "stand still" and wrongly argued that the Bible teaches that the sun must orbit the earth. This was, however, a misreading of Scripture and the scientists were proved right. Citing this example, many evangelicals today are prepared to concede the Bible's entire teaching of creation to the supposedly infallible results of science. Instead, we ought to be willing to examine our teachings to ensure that we have not mistakenly interpreted God's Word. Then, once we are sure of the Bible's teaching on its own terms, we must follow the priority stated fifty years ago by E. J. Young: "general revelation is to be interpreted by special revelation, nature by Scripture, 'science' by the Bible."[65]

Non-Literal Approaches to Genesis 1

Until about three hundred years ago, Christians were virtually unanimous in reading Genesis 1 as presenting creation in six literal days. Under the pressure of scientific opposition, this situation has shifted so that today large percentages of Bible believers have adopted non-literal views of the creation days. This change occurred not because of more careful Bible study, "but as a result of accepting the truth claims of scientists over the propositional revelation of Scripture."[66] Today, there are a variety of theories that see Genesis 1 in non-literal ways in order to lessen or remove the conflict with science. The three most prominent theories among evangelicals are the age–day concordance theory, the analogical days view, and the Framework Hypothesis.

The *age-day concordance view* begins by noting that the Hebrew word for "day" (*yom*) does not necessarily mean a twenty-four hour period but can also describe broader periods of time. Conceding scientific findings of an extremely old earth, this theory posits that the days of creation may each have consisted of millions or billions of years. Taken this way, the chronology and sequence of creation in Genesis 1 may be seen as in concordance with scientific theories about the development of the cosmos. Biblical support is seen in Peter's teaching that "with the Lord one day is as a thousand years, and a thousand years as one day" (2 Peter 3:8).

The problems to this view are serious. First, we should usually take a word's normal meaning unless urged otherwise by the context. There is no question that the normal meaning of the Hebrew noun *yom* is a twenty-four hour day. The context of Genesis 1 agrees with this view, describing each day with the words, "there was evening and there was morning" (Genesis 1:5). Moreover, if Moses wished to convey the idea of creation ages, there are better Hebrew words, such as *dor* and *olam*. A further problem is that conceiving of the days as ages does not really produce agreement with science, since the sequence and order in Genesis 1 remains at odds with scientific theories.[67] Finally, Peter was not teaching that the days of creation are long ages but simply that God experiences time differently than we do.

A modified approach to the age-day theory is known as the *analogical day theory*. This approach adds to the prior theory by considering the seventh day. First, it is assumed that since Genesis 2:2–3 does not conclude with the "evening" and "morning" formula, the seventh day is an eternal age without end. By analogy, if the seventh day is an endless age, the earlier six days may also be ages. The problem with this view, along with the problems already noted with the age-day theory, is its assumption. Young notes: "There is no Scriptural warrant ever … for the idea that the seventh day is eternal."[68] It is true that the seventh day is a *symbol* for God's eternal rest (see Hebrews 4:3–10). But in the Bible, a symbol and its fulfillment are not the same. There is nothing in the text to identify the seventh day as longer than the other six, so that the analogy is without biblical support.

Building on these two non-literal views of Genesis 1 is the increasingly popular *Framework Hypothesis*. This approach follows three lines of reasoning to argue that Genesis 1 does not present a chronology at all. Henri Blocher asserts, "The author's intention is not to supply us with a chronology of origins ... He wishes to bring out certain themes and provide a theology of the sabbath."[69]

The first tenet of the Framework Hypothesis is that Genesis 1 should be considered as poetry rather than an historical account because of its obvious literary craftsmanship. There is, for instance, a pattern of threes, sevens, and tens for the major themes: God blesses three times, says "and it was so" seven times, and we read "God said," and "let there be" ten times each. Having already assumed that the days are analogous to long ages, and noting the repetition of "evening" and "morning," Meredith Kline classifies Genesis 1 as semi-poetic, "in the epic tradition." This structure, he argues, should cause us to view Genesis 1 as "figurative" rather than a "genuinely historical record of the origins of the universe."[70]

A second argument draws from Genesis 2, which is said to operate by ordinary providence, that is, it involves normal rather than supernatural processes. Genesis 2:5 says that "no bush of the field was yet in the land and no small plant of the field had yet sprung up—for the LORD God had not caused it to rain on the land, and there was no man to work the ground." Kline argues that this is a parallel account of the third day in Genesis 1:11, where the earth is made to "sprout vegetation ... and fruit trees bearing fruit." This shows, Kline argues, that the plant growth of Genesis 1:11 took place by ordinary means, requiring rain to fall and man to garden, all of which could not have taken place in a twenty-four hour day. Moreover, it is argued that Genesis 2 shows a variety of activity that could not have occurred on a literal sixth day. Adam was created and placed in the garden. God made the woman from Adam's rib. Along the way, God brought "every beast of the field and every bird of the heavens and brought them to the man to see what he would call them" (Genesis 2:19). Mark Ross asks: "If we take seriously that Adam did this with every beast of the field and every bird of the sky, is it conceivable that he accomplished all this in the space of one day?"[71] Since the description in Genesis 2 of the activity within the creation days could not have happened in twenty-four hours, the literal view of the days is contradicted.

The third argument stems from the structure of the six creation days, which reveals not a chronological but a thematic relationship. Days one and four, two and five, and three and six are paired in such a way that God first creates an environment and then provides occupants. Or, as Kline puts it, God provides *kingdoms* and then places *kings*: on day 1, God creates night and day and, on day 4, he places lights to rule them; day 2 separates the sky from the waters of the earth and day 5 fills them with swimming and flying creatures; day 3 provides the dry earth and day 6 places beasts on the land along with mankind.[72] Based on this literary structure, Genesis 1 cannot be seen to present a chronology for creation, but rather a poetic literary structure.

The Framework Hypothesis makes impressive points.

However, each of its arguments fails under careful analysis.[73] First, despite the careful literary crafting, Genesis 1 is not poetry but rather possesses the normal characteristics of historical prose narrative. In particular, it does not have the parallelism demanded by Hebrew poetry. Notice the parallel phrases in the Song of Moses, celebrating Israel's passage through the Red Sea:

> I will sing to the LORD, for he has triumphed gloriously;
> the horse and his rider he has thrown into the sea.
> The LORD is my strength and my song,
> and he has become my salvation;
> this is my God, and I will praise him,
> my father's God, and I will exalt him (Exodus 15:1–2).

Now consider the account of the first day in Genesis 1:3–5:

> And God said, "Let there be light," and there was light. And God saw that the light was good. And God separated the light from the darkness. God called the light Day, and the darkness he called Night. And there was evening and there was morning, the first day.

The reality is that Genesis 1 bears little resemblance to Old Testament poetry but rather shows all the marks of historical prose narrative.[74] Furthermore, even if Genesis 1 is poetic or semi-poetic, this would not preclude it from recording true history, as the Song of Moses shows with its accurate record of Pharaoh's defeat.

Second, the Framework Hypothesis wrongly relates Genesis 2 to Genesis 1. The Genesis 2 account begins, "These are the generations of the heavens and the earth" (Genesis 2:4). This formula occurs ten times in Genesis, marking off successive narratives. This means that Genesis 2 is not a parallel creation account that contradicts Genesis 1, but rather the record of what happened afterwards, starting on the sixth day, when God was interacting with Adam and Eve in the Garden. Moreover, there is no reason to doubt that the events of Genesis 2 could have taken place on a single day, especially since God himself was immediately performing most of them. As for the animals brought to Adam, the various "kinds" of species had not yet experienced variation, so there would not likely have been thousands. Nor was it necessary for Adam to study every species, since God was giving him a sample to prove that among the beasts "there was not found a helper fit for him" (Genesis 2:20). There is thus no sound basis for Genesis 2 to deny a literal reading of chapter 1.

Third, the literary structure of the creation days observed by Kline and others provides valuable insights. We have previously noted that creation and salvation both involve God creating a home and then providing a people. But on close examination, the strict literary framework breaks down and does not disprove the validity of the historical chronology in Genesis 1. As Noel Weeks writes: "The claim that careful structure in the composition means that the passage is not to be taken literally is nothing more than a claim. How do we know that structure and literalness are incompatible?"[75]

The common thread to all the non-literal interpretation of Genesis 1 is that they reinterpret the text for the primary cause of avoiding conflict with secular science, including the theory of evolution. Henri Blocher frankly admits this motivation: "The rejection of all the theories accepted by the scientists requires considerable bravado ... current opinions, built on the studies of thousands of research scientists who keep a very close eye on one another, continue to look very probable."[76] It should not, however, be the Christian's goal to accommodate the Bible to the theories of men, especially those fundamentally at odds with the message of Scripture.

Evidence for the Literal Chronology of Genesis 1

Having rejected the non-literal accounts of Genesis 1, we need to give solid evidence for a literal chronology of creation. Let me provide five lines of evidence.

The first two have already been mentioned. First, the *genre* of Genesis 1 is straightforward historical prose narrative, not poetry, however elaborate its construction may be. Its basic structure is the same as the other 49 chapters of Genesis and, as history, it should be read as a record of authentic events. Geerhardus Vos observes the danger to the entire Bible if Genesis 1 can be discarded as history: "If the creation history is an allegory, then the narrative concerning the fall and everything further that follows can also be allegory."[77] Derek Kidner thus comments "that the author shows no consciousness of speaking otherwise than literally."[78] Second, the Hebrew *grammar* of Genesis 1, with the *waw consecutive* construction of "*waw* + verb" marks a sequence of events wherever this grammatical structure is found in the Old Testament.[79]

Third, the *numbering* of the creation days identifies them as normal, twenty-four hour days. Joseph Pipa writes: "the use of 'day' with the ordinal number demands a sequential reading … When an ordinal number is used with *yom*, not one example of non-sequence can be found."[80] Thus, the fact that

Genesis 1 numbers the days as first, second, and so on, gives the normal impression of ordinary days.

Fourth, we note that the *context* of the days is marked by the words "evening and morning." This signifies the period of darkness and the breaking of dawn that ends the day which began with the creation of light. Critics respond that "evening and morning" presuppose the existence of the sun and the earth's rotation on its axis, none of which had yet been created. In answering, the Christian does not at all deny the supernaturalism that is involved throughout these creation events. The reality is, however, that Bible presents creation in normal, twenty-four hour day periods.

Fifth, when the Bible later looks back on Genesis' creation story, it regards the events as historically literal. Paul pointed out that in the beginning, God said, "Let light shine out of darkness" (2 Corinthians 4:6), validating the historical claim of Genesis 1:3. In Matthew 19:4, Jesus spoke of Adam and Eve as historical persons. Psalm 33 corroborates the claim of Genesis 1: "By the word of the LORD the heavens were made, and by the breath of his mouth all their host" (Psalm 33:6).

Most telling is the language of the Fourth Commandment, establishing the weekly Sabbath, which includes this explanation: "For in six days the LORD made heaven and earth, the sea, and all that is in them, and rested on the seventh day" (Exodus 20:11). The logic of this command is that we must do as God himself did. We are to work for six literal days each week, resting on the seventh, to imitate what God did on the original days of creation.

Armed with this evidence—Genesis 1's historical genre, its

narrative grammar, the numbering of the days, the context of evening and morning, together with the agreement of the rest of Scripture—Christians may be confident in reading the days of Genesis 1 as literal, twenty-four hour periods. Instructed by God's Word, we stand humbly but confidently before the contrary teaching of science.

How, then, do we answer science's teaching that the universe is billions of years old rather than the thousands of years indicated by Scripture? Some Christian scientists answer with Bible-based scientific theories that support Genesis 1. Consider, for instance, the light that shines from the nearby Andromeda galaxy, which science says has traveled 2.5 million years, based on a constant speed of light. But Christian scientist C. Stuart Patterson presents evidence that the speed of light has actually been slowing down. If the speed of light was exponentially faster at the dawn of creation, the resulting revision to science would agree with Scripture.[81]

Most Bible readers lack the scientific competence to make such arguments. But there are other ways to reduce or explain the conflict. Vern Poythress argues a "mature creation" approach, noting that Adam seems to have been created in a mature, adult form, rather than growing from infancy. By analogy, there is no reason why God could not have created the universe with a mature appearance, including light already in motion from distant stars. "If so," Poythress writes, "the age estimates from modern science, such as 4.5 billion years for the earth and 14 billion years for the universe, are simply coherent instances of apparent age."[82]

This kind of reasoning, together with alternative scientific theories, may help to bridge the gap between Bible believers and scientists, although the secular hostility to Christianity makes this difficult in practice. Nonetheless, Christians should stand steadfastly and confidently on God's Word, knowing, as Psalm 119:130 says, "The unfolding of your words gives light."

Creation and the Gospel

As we conclude our analysis of the creation days, we may return to Augustine's original question: is the Bible designed to create mathematicians or Christians? The answer is that in this chapter we have done virtually no science but have instead considered how to handle the Bible correctly. Rightly interpreting Scripture is, of course, of the greatest importance to believers. We began by pointing out the superiority of God's Word compared to any mere human authority, and we have sought to understand Genesis 1 on its own terms. Only having read the Bible faithfully do we consider the claims of the world and seek to answer its objections.

It hardly needs to be said that this same discipline and faithfulness is essential to our reading the Gospel accounts of Jesus Christ. For the world that rejects biblical creation and a literal Adam and Eve is not better disposed to the Bible's record of Christ. The same naturalistic secularism has assailed Jesus' virgin birth, miracles, sin-atoning death, bodily resurrection, ascension to heaven and imminent return to earth. Moreover, the very kinds of arguments made by Christians to discount the historicity of Genesis 1 are used by unbelievers to allegorize the Gospels, which like Genesis involve careful literary construction and dramatic elements. The Gospel of John, for instance, involves intense literary structuring, highlighting exodus motifs, the feast schedule of

Old Testament Israel, and the "I am" statements of Christ. It features dramatic events and miraculous claims. It concludes in the bodily resurrection of Christ which is ridiculed by today's science. Does this mean that John's Gospel is not historically true? And if it is not history, but a mere literary structure, what is left of Christian faith?

Christian theology relies on the truthfulness of biblical history, for creation as well as the cross. Therefore, if Christians accept a version of our origins that is at odds with Genesis 1, we have not made a tactically wise compromise but have recast the grand story of the entire Bible. Without a historical Genesis 1 there is no literal Adam and Eve. Without our first parents there is no fall into sin as the great problem of life. In that case, the mission ascribed to Jesus in dying for our forgiveness bears no meaning and little relevance to a world that is simply about something else. The Bible's message of creation-fall-redemption starts with an historical account of creation that is simply indispensable to our faith.

Augustine was right in asserting that Genesis was written to create Christians, not mathematicians. And according to the New Testament, the story of Jesus begins in Genesis 1: "In the beginning was the Word" (John 1:1-2). At the Bible's end, Jesus wrapped up all history, saying, "I am the first and the last, and the living one. I died, and behold I am alive forevermore" (Revelation 1:17-18). These are historical claims, presented by Scripture together with all of the Bible's claims, which we set before a skeptical world. We proclaim them, trusting that Christ, through the power by which he spoke all things into being in the days of creation, will speak the word of the new birth into the hearts of men and

women, so that by believing the truth of God's Word they
will be saved.

7   *Making and Separating*

Genesis 1:6–10

*And God said, "Let there be an expanse in the midst of
the waters, and let it separate the waters from the waters"*
(Genesis 1:6).

WHEN SECULAR WRITERS SPEAK ABOUT THE UNIVERSE THEY
often emphasize how small and insignificant is the earth and,
by extension, the human race. Richard Dawkins describes the
earth as "the tiny stage on which we play out our lives—our
speck of debris from the cosmic explosion."[83] Carl Sagan
described it as "a tiny speck of rock and metal, shining
feebly by reflected sunlight."[84] The worldview arising from
these claims is necessarily one that devalues human life and
experience.

Genesis 1 bears exactly the opposite message. One feature of
the Bible's creation account is its striking earth-centeredness.
The very first day of creation is measured in earth-terms:
"evening and morning, day one." Especially on the second and
third days, God constructs the universe with a focus on the
earth. Far from our experience lacking any significance in the
grand cosmos, Genesis sees the universe finding its relevance
in terms of the earth which God has made. Whatever the
earth is to contemporary atheists, to God it is not "debris"

that "shines feebly." Instead, Genesis 1 presents the earth as a jewel that, if not at the physical center of the universe, is at the center of God's purpose and plan for history.

An Expanse Between the Waters

The language of Genesis 1:6, on the second day of creation, has caused a great deal of study: "And God said, 'Let there be an expanse in the midst of the waters, and let it separate the waters from the waters.'" To liberal scholars, who are ever eager to show the so-called "mythical" nature of Genesis 1, this statement supplies precious ammunition. They point out that in describing Noah's flood, Moses says, "the windows of the heavens were opened" (Genesis 7:11). This shows, they argue, that he believed the sky was a great sea (the sky being blue, you see), not recognizing a metaphor when they see it. Moreover, the Hebrew word for "expanse" (*raqia*) is used in Job 37:18 to describe the sky as a tin mirror. Put together, Moses' creation account is relegated to a mythology in which the sky is a metal dome holding back the cosmic ocean, somewhat like the dykes of Holland keeping back the North Atlantic waters.

Before we toss our Bibles onto a pile of Mesopotamian fiction and start teaching evolution, we should note some contrary evidence. It turns out that *raqia* does not mean a metal dome but comes from a verb meaning "to stretch out." It is sometimes used of tin or other metals because of the way they are beaten and flattened. But elsewhere it is used as a curtain, such as when Isaiah 40:22 says that God "stretches out the heavens like a curtain."[85] Moreover, it is very doubtful that the Israelites would have simply imbibed the cosmology of their pagan neighbors, since their religion strongly emphasized the need to separate from idolaters. Instead, the evidence suggests that Moses and Israel had a relatively sophisticated understanding of their planet. When God made the sun and the moon on the fourth day, he "set them in" the *raqia* (Genesis 1:17). Genesis 1:20 sees the flying creatures soaring within the *raqia*. This doesn't sound like a metal dome, does it, since it portrays depth within the sky? Likewise, when Moses spoke of the "windows of the heavens," this was a figurative depiction of the deluge that was falling from the sky.

The best way to understand the *raqia* or *expanse* of Genesis 1:6 is as a barrier spread out by God to separate the waters of earth (seas) from the waters above (sky). So the *raqia* describes the atmosphere in which our clouds hover. This was a remarkable thing for God to have done and so far as we know it is unique in the observable universe, making life possible on our wonderful planet. How far from an "insignificant speck" is this world like no other! In all its extensive investigation, science has never discovered another remotely like it.

God made the atmosphere to "separate the waters from the waters" (Genesis 1:6), the sky separating "the waters that were under the expanse from the waters that were above the expanse" (Genesis 1:7). If we doubt that there are waters above, we need only look upward on a rainy day. The legions of clouds flout in the atmosphere, holding and sometimes pouring down vast quantities of water. In this way, the second day witnessed an advance in God's creation of the earth's ecosystem, including natural laws that govern winds and clouds. William Still comments on the enormity of this achievement:

The separation of the waters, under from over, provides the vital atmosphere—"that mysterious blending of oxygen, nitrogen, and other elementary gases which constitute the earth's envelope of air"—in which alone we can survive. The marvel is that the clouds are supported upon "a substance so light that on certain days we are scarcely conscious of its presence, yet so powerful as to be able to bear upon its bosom billions of tons of water evaporated from the ocean."[86]

The second day of creation may not seem as exciting as the first, but how important it was: "And God called the expanse Heaven. And there was evening and there was morning, the second day" (Genesis 1:8).

Making and Separating

It is worth noting that Genesis 1:7 uses a word for "made" (Hebrew, *asah*) that is different from the word "create" in Genesis 1:1. The idea is that God is now working with the material he previously made. Notice as well that in contrast with the creation myths of other ancient cultures, God's creation involves construction rather than conflict. The Babylonian creation epic *Enuma Elish* sees the god Marduk slaying the dragon Tiamat and casting her tail into the heavens to make the sky. But there is no such warfare as God creates, makes, and shapes. Meredith Kline writes: "There is no serious suggestion in Scripture of the existence of divine adversaries with whom the creating God had to contend."[87] Creation is the masterwork of divine architecture and construction, God designing a theater for the display of his glory and a stage for the outworking of his sovereign plan.

If we reflect on the structure of God's construction we will find a prevalence of binary couplets. This means that the creation was structured with a series of two opposite and complementary parts. On day one, God created light and darkness, day and night. On day two, God made heaven and earth. On day four we see the sun and the moon. On the sixth day God created mankind in binary sexes: "male and female he created them" (Genesis 1:27). As the Bible progresses we continue to find what Peter Jones has called a "two-ist" structure.[88] The biblical worldview is thus organized as heaven and earth, male and female, good and evil, faith and unbelief, life and death, true and false, salvation and damnation. At the foundation of this binary structure is the basic declaration of Genesis 1:1 with the binary reality of the Creator and his creation: "In the beginning, God created the heavens and earth."

Not only does God make things in pairs, but he then orders the creation by making a clear differentiation between them. Genesis 1:4 introduces the word *separation* (Hebrew, *badal*) as God's way of shaping the universe. Verse 6 says that God made the *raqia* to separate the waters above and below. All told, "separate" occurs five times in Genesis 1, marking it as the primary means of God's ordering (Genesis 1:4, 6, 7, 14, 18). The point is that God makes a clear distinction between opposites and gives to each a proper sphere. The Christian and biblical worldview, therefore, proceeding from Genesis 1:1 with its Creator-creature distinction, is one that sees a divine order to the world, with clear categories and distinctions which God made and declares good. This binary structure is the mark of biblical theism, in which truth is received from God as opposed to error, through faith versus unbelief, cultivated in obedience rather than rebellion, with an aim to life instead of death.

This pattern reinforces our idea of Genesis 1 as key to a biblical and Christian worldview. The Bible's first verse declares that there is a Creator who is not part of the creation and the creation is not part of God. Moses wrote this in a polytheistic world which believed that "all is one." The false gods were part of the creation and their worship was a way of manipulating nature. In worshiping one god, you sought to bring rain. Worshiping another god increased your chances of fertility. Another god brought happiness and yet another power. Idolatry was, in this way, a worship of the creation in the place of the Creator. According to the apostle Paul, this idolatry is at the very heart of sin: "Claiming to be wise, they became fools, and exchanged the glory of the immortal God for images resembling mortal man and birds and animals and creeping things" (Romans 1:22–23).

This reflection shows that the opposite of biblical monotheism is not atheism but rather pantheism; whereas the Bible proclaims God on the one hand and nature on the other, pantheistic paganism proclaims that nature is god. Having rejected the Creator-creature distinction of Genesis 1:1, paganism subsequently rejects the Bible's further distinctions. Henri Blocher comments: "When we study non-biblical religions, we constantly discover a fascination with intermixture and a kind of longing for a universal dissolution of differences."[89] What God has separated in creation, paganism collapses in rebellion: life and death, true and false, male and female, the Creator and creation are merged together into one.

Idolatry's rejection of the binary structure in biblical creation might seem like ancient history if pagan one-ism was not the worldview seeking to replace Christianity in Western culture today. Recent decades have seen an intellectual quest taking the form of deconstruction. Jacques Derrida, its founder, stated as his purpose to "deconstruct the dualisms and hierarchies embedded in Western thinking," which he regards as "false polarities" to be destroyed.[90]

This neo-pagan agenda proceeds from the supposed removal of the biblical God. With no Creator to make and rule, there is no grand story or meaning, leaving each individual to make his or her own story and determine his or her own meaning. There is no truth, no heaven, no gender, and no purpose other than that which each person decides individually. All is one so that structure, categories, order, and obligation are removed. This pagan one-ist worldview permeates our culture today, especially in the arts. John Lennon wrote its anthem, singing: "Imagine there's no heaven/It's easy if you try/No hell below us/Above us, only sky."[91] Movies, plays, and novels similarly present a world in which good and evil are virtually impossible to tell apart, in which there is no meaningful difference between men and women, and in which the only real liars are those pitiful fools who still believe in absolute truth. Perhaps the classic expression of this neo-pagan hubris was given by George Lucas in *Star Wars 3*, when the mystic Jedi Yoda assigned Christians to the "Dark Side," saying, "Only the Sith are absolutists."

The problem with neo-pagan one-ism is that its original premise is false (sorry, Yoda!). Contrary to the news reports, God is not dead; the reports of his demise, as Winston

Churchill once said of himself, are premature! There remains a single God who is the Creator of all things, and who structured the creation according to his own will: light and darkness, heaven and earth, day and night, male and female. The witness of Genesis 1:1 stands: "In the beginning, God."

To accept the Bible and believe in God therefore means to follow Genesis 1 forward in accepting the creation as God has made it. The problem in the church today, therefore, is not that Christians fail to get on board the neo-pagan agenda, but rather that too many profess faith in the Bible and yet accommodate the one-ist worldview of pagan culture. It is from the idolatrous script that we are reading when we downplay the distinctions between true and false, male and female, life and death, the church and the world. To receive in faith Genesis 1's witness about God and his creation calls us to be people who stand for truth against error, defend life against death, cultivate biblical standards of gender and sexuality against gender confusion and sexual immorality, and live by faith in the face of unbelief. To live in such a way today is to be completely out of synch with our suddenly pagan culture, just as Moses and his Israelite readers were out of step with the ancient world through which they sojourned to the land of God's promise. It is to be worshipers of the living God rather than the dead idols of the cultural elites.

The Good Earth

Genesis 1:9 brings us to the third day of creation, where the work of day two is completed: "And God said, 'Let the waters under the heavens be gathered together into one place, and let the dry land appear.' And it was so." Having separated the waters above (the clouds) from the earth, God now gathers the waters below so that dry land may surface.

It is not clear exactly how God caused the land to appear, whether he drained the waters or caused the land to spring up in the seas. Biblical teaching elsewhere suggests the latter. Job 38:8 says that the "mountains rose" in the seas. Psalm 104:8 paints a similar picture: "The mountains rose, the valleys sank down to the place that you appointed for them." Up until this point, the earth apparently consisted only of water, so it seems that God did some molecular rearrangement in order to make silicon and carbon as the building blocks for the rocks and minerals of the rising land. 2 Peter 3:5 agrees with this picture: "the earth was formed out of water and through water by the word of God."

John Currid summarizes God's achievement: "The fundamental construction of the cosmos—sky, earth and sea—is now established. In other words, the physical structure is finished, and it awaits God's acts of filling with things to dwell in it."[92] Unless we presuppose that these events could only take place over millions of years there is no reason to doubt that God could have accomplished this work quickly (as we conceive it) by his omnipotent power. The impact of such sudden upheaval on the geological record would be immense, perhaps accounting for the apparent contradictions between science and the Bible in the genealogical record.

As we gaze on God's work of making the earth for our habitation, we should note that God rules by his own power and according to his own Word. The sovereignty of God is written large over the entirety of the creation account, especially in these verses where we learn of God wreathing the earth with its water-laden atmosphere and summoning continents out of the primordial sea. The implication is that God possesses every right and ability to rule the world which he made in his own way. The laws of nature continue to function in the manner that God fixed them to sustain and nurture life on earth. While there are small shifts along the line of the seashore, it remains true that God's boundary between the sea and the land holds fast. The drumbeat of Genesis 1 continues to be heard today: "God said ... And it was so" (Genesis 1:9). This marks "the absolute authority of the One who speaks; nothing resists his command, everything bows to his decrees."[93] Thus the Word of God, which effects God's purpose, is as certain as his sovereign will which shaped the earth in the dawn of creation.

The prophet Isaiah made the power of God's Word a point of emphasis as he challenged his generation to trust in the Lord's promises. Facing mounting unbelief and ungodliness, he called on the people to repent and believe, trusting God to grant a salvation they would fail to achieve by their own efforts. "Israel is saved by the LORD with everlasting salvation; you shall not be put to shame or confounded to all eternity," he claimed (Isaiah 45:17). But on what basis can such confidence in God be established? Isaiah answered by looking back to the sovereign power of God's Word in forming the heavens and the earth: "For thus says the LORD, who created the heavens (he is God!), who formed the earth and made it (he established it; he did not create it empty, he formed it to be inhabited!): 'I am the LORD, and there is no other'" (Isaiah 45:18).

When you open your Bible today and consider God's claims,

commands, and promises, you should remember that this same Word separated the heaven and the earth and made the dry land appear amidst the seas. The Word of God will continue to be mighty and true, and the Creator who ruled the earth's first days by his Word will rule them all, to the very last. "'I am the Alpha and the Omega,' says the Lord God, 'who is and who was and who is to come, the Almighty'" (Revelation 1:8).

God continued to exercise his sovereignty by naming what he made: "God called the dry land Earth, and the waters that were gathered together he called Seas" (Genesis 1:10). At this point, midway through day three, God looks on his work and declares his satisfaction: "And God saw that it was good" (Genesis 1:10).

It is often observed that day two did not end with God's word of approval. This fact has prompted some biblical humorists to quip that not even God considers Monday to be good! A better explanation is that the work of day two was completed on day three. At that point God looked on the heavens above and the earth below and declared that it was good. Umberto Cassuto writes: "Now that the work of the water was completed and the world had assumed its proper tripartite form of Heaven, Earth and Sea, it is possible to declare, that it is good."[94] By our standards, what God accomplished on the second and third days of creation staggers the mind in contemplation of his greatness. R. Kent Hughes writes of it: "The earth, warmed by light, was now robed in blue and dappled with clouds floating over a sparkling sea. The picture is increasingly inviting."[95] Indeed, the God of the heavens and the earth is not only great, but he is wonderfully good.

Blessing by the Word

As we appreciate the astonishing achievement of God's Word in creating heaven and earth we are better prepared to rejoice in the greater glory of the gospel as it tells us of God's redemption from our sin in Jesus Christ. The New Testament frequently refers to our salvation in creation terms. For instance, Paul writes: "if anyone is in Christ, he is a new creation" (2 Corinthians 5:17). This being the case, our study of God's working in Genesis 1 finds its echo in our salvation through faith in Jesus.

Consider the great phrases that are repeated over and over throughout the creation record of Genesis 1: "And God said [ten times] ... And it was so [seven times] ... And God blessed it [three times] ... And it was good [seven times]." These statements mark a chorus or refrain within the grand historical narrative. That "God said and it was so" is still seen every evening and morning as the days roll forward to their appointed end.

This Genesis 1 way of thinking prepares us for the pattern of salvation through faith in God's Word that recurs in the New Testament. God purposed to bring blessing to the earth and in creation it was all good. The Bible will go on to speak of the entry of sin and our alienation as sinners from the blessing of God. Yet God's blessing remained on the earth through his Word. Out of this purpose to bless, God sent his Son to remedy the stain of sin that separated heaven and earth more completely than did the original expanse in the creation sky.

So God's Son came from heaven to earth, and as his blood fell to the ground from the cross, God's Word was fulfilled in restoring blessing to those who believe.

God has said. It is so. God's blessing is upon his gospel Word. We receive that Word in faith, trusting in God's Son, Jesus Christ, and then living so as to reflect Genesis 1, honoring God's order in a world made for his glory. And while ungodly voices declare this glorious world as an insignificant speck and a stage for meaningless lives, we by God's Word receive the benediction once spoken over the heavens and earth. Through faith, God says of our salvation: "And it was good."

8   *Creation versus Evolution*

Genesis 1:11–13

And God said, "Let the earth sprout vegetation, plants yielding seed, and fruit trees bearing fruit in which is their seed, each according to its kind, on the earth." And it was so (Genesis 1:11).

As we continue to study Genesis 1, we have covered enough ground that we should take some time to recap. We have noted the vast significance of Genesis 1:1 to the Christian worldview. "In the beginning, God created" identifies God as eternal, transcendent, and separate from the things he has made. It tells us that there is a purpose to history that comes from its Maker, who can be relied upon to rule all that he created by his mere word. Genesis 1:1 notes our accountability as creatures to the Creator and our dependence on him for all things.

We saw in Genesis 1:2 that God looks on the creation in terms of the home he is providing and the people who will inhabit it. By verse 3, we have encountered God in his triune persons: the Father ordaining and speaking, the Spirit hovering and empowering, and the Son achieving as the Divine Word. Beginning the six creation days, we noted that Genesis 1 reads as an historical narrative that recounts actual though unique events. On days one and two, God began ordering his creation by separating into binary complements—heaven and earth, light and darkness, sea and land, etc.—each of which God places in its proper category.

By day three, God has already separated the sea from the land, and now in Genesis 1:11–13 he fills the ground with plant life. The key point in these verses involves the principle of reproduction as God made it. Here, the biblical doctrine of creation collides with the secular theory of evolution. Did God create the various creatures, causing them to reproduce only within their kinds? Or did the various organisms arise through a random process of gradual evolution from lower to higher forms?

Sprouting with Vegetation

When the third day has been completed, God has filled the earth with plant life: "And God said, 'Let the earth sprout vegetation, plants yielding seed, and fruit trees bearing fruit in which is their seed, each according to its kind, on the earth.' And it was so" (Genesis 1:11). Here we have God covering the ground which earlier that day he had gathered amidst the waters of earth.

Genesis says that God caused the earth to sprout vegetation of two kinds: one with the seed on the plant and the other with seed inside fruit (see also Genesis 1:29). John Currid writes: "These two terms represent all agricultural and horticultural plant life" on earth.[96]

Apparently, the plants and trees arose from the ground whole. When the perennial question is asked, "Which came first, the chicken or the egg?" or in this case, "the plant or the seed?" the Bible's answer is the plant (hence, the chicken). God made the plants with seed. The emphasis is therefore placed on the reproductive capacity that God built into plant life: "The earth brought forth vegetation, plants yielding seed according to their own kinds, and trees bearing fruit in which is their seed, each according to its kind" (Genesis 1:12). The point of seed, whether inside or outside of fruit, is the plants' ability to reproduce by what would now be a natural process. God in this way "grants the means of self-perpetuation to various species and orders of creation."[97] This same principle will be extended to animal life and then humans. Once God created life with a capacity to reproduce, each kind of being subsequently has both a supernatural and natural origin. Plants come from seed, but ultimately Psalm 147:8 is right to say that it is God who "makes grass grow on the hills."

In Genesis 1, everything is created with a purpose. God made the earth so that plants could grow on it. He then made plants so that animals would have food (Genesis 1:29–30). He created the animals for the dominion of man. And God created mankind—male and female—in order to bear his own image on the earth. The various kinds of plants therefore find a divine purpose in the service that they provide to higher beings and ultimately in the contribution they make to the glory of God.

As before, the language of creation emphasizes God's own will and Word, resulting in his personal approval. "And God said, 'Let the earth sprout vegetation'" (Genesis 1:11). Here, the Bible expressly refutes the idea of "Mother Earth," as if the capacity for life was generated by nature itself. True, the earth produces plant life, but only at God's will and command, however natural the process may seem in its repetitions. The bounty of the earth is a cause not merely to rejoice in the wonder of nature but also to glory in the goodness of God. No wonder that God looked upon his work of the third day, which completed his preparation of the earth for the inhabitants to come, seeing "that it was good" (Genesis 1:12).

Assessing Scientific Claims for Evolution

Over the last 150 years, an alternative to biblical creation has arisen in the form of the secular theory of evolution. Evolution denies that the various creatures appeared by God's creative design and act. Instead, each species gradually developed from lower forms by a random process of natural selection. Ever since the publication of Charles Darwin's *The Origin of the Species* in 1859, evolution has served primarily as a scientific justification for the removal of God. As Phillip Johnson has written, once evolution is accepted as a "fact," this means "that all living things are the produce of mindless material forces such as chemical laws, natural selection, and random variation. So God is totally out of the picture."[98] Julian Huxley, a leading evolution proponent, cited this as evolution's great virtue:

> In the evolutionary pattern of thought there is no longer either need or room for the supernatural. The earth was not created: it evolved. So did all the animals and plants that inhabit it, including our human selves, mind and soul as well as brain and body. So did religion.[99]

Given the blatant opposition of evolution to biblical creation, it may seem surprising that some Christians seek to accommodate evolution into their faith. The reason is the claim that evolution has been "proven" as a "fact," and the cultural shame attached to any so bold as to deny it. In avoiding this contradictory position, it is helpful to know that evolution is far from proved as being true, despite sensational media reports to that effect.

Consider the oft-cited 2010 report from the University of California at San Francisco that humans and chimpanzees share ninety-nine per cent of their DNA. The implication is made that mankind is only very slightly different from chimps and that we obviously arose from a common ancestry. This kind of evidence is intimidating to Christians, who find it intellectually difficult to hold a biblical view in the face of such claims. Before abandoning the Bible, however, Christians are wise to investigate the actual study being cited. What the media report did not say is that the ninety-nine per cent figure was arrived at only after large portions of the DNA were excluded from the study, on the grounds that they were so fundamentally different. It turns out that no less than twenty-eight per cent of the total DNA was excluded from the study on this basis, so that with this and other factors included, a more accurate figure would state that humans and chimpanzees share sixty-eight per cent of their DNA.[100]

This example highlights a characteristic feature of scientific claims in support of evolution: the reported results are manufactured by the way data is selected and organized. Another important matter is the prominent role of presuppositions in interpreting the data. Today's science operates on the assumption of the gradual evolution of species. So if humans and apes have shared DNA, the assumption is made that the common DNA is evidence of a shared past development. But the DNA proves nothing of the sort: it is the assumption that is producing the conclusion. The Bible provides another explanation for why humans and lower animals share DNA: because God made them with similarities. It turns out that the great majority of the DNA shared by humans and chimps has to do with the basic chemical machinery within cells, proving merely that humans and chimpanzees are both mammals. This claim is no threat to the Bible, which describes both animals and humans as "living creatures" (Genesis 1:24; 2:7). Moreover, there are biblical reasons why God made mankind with biological similarities to the lower animals. Vern Poythress writes: "Man made in the image of God is supreme over the animals (Genesis 1:28), but he also has a definite solidarity with them."[101] Thus God created the animals to have considerable biological similarity with the human race so they could work together.

Upon examination, it turns out, a scientific finding reported as proving the evolution of mankind from apes provides no basis for that finding at all. The same might be said for other human genome studies that claim mankind is hundreds of thousands of years old or that human DNA could not have emerged from a single set of parents. It is typical of these studies, as of all scientific studies, that decisions made regarding the inclusion or exclusion of data determine the results and that assumptions often having little to do with science govern the conclusions.[102]

The Bible and Evolution

The question that Christians must ask is how the theory of

evolution squares with the Bible's account of creation. There are several lines of argument that show the two approaches to be fundamentally and irreconcilably opposed.

First, notice that while evolution ascribes the origin of species to a purposeless biological process, the Bible declares God as the Creator who personally made all things according to his will. Some counter that God may have chosen to create the species by means of evolution. The problem with this assertion is the account of Genesis 1. This is why some scholars argue against the historical validity of Genesis 1, describing it as poetic literature that teaches theology but not historical truth. We have previously refuted this claim, noting that both at the level of grammar and literary type, Genesis 1 is standard Old Testament historical narrative.[103] If the truth claims of Genesis 1 may be dismissed by simply declaring its theology as non-historical, there is no chapter in the Bible that cannot be similarly dismissed when it conflicts with secularist dogma.

A particular problem in accommodating Genesis 1 to evolution is the specific emphasis given in verses 11 and 12 to the manner of reproduction as God designed it. God called forth the vegetation, both fruit and non-fruit-bearing plants, "each according to its kind." It is probably too narrow a definition to say that the "kinds" of Genesis 1 correspond to what scientists define today as "species." More broadly, the kinds approximate the *genus*, major families in which related species exist. For instance, canis is the genus for the dog family, including *canis lupus*, containing wolves and domestic dogs, and *canis latrans*, which is the coyote. Within a genus there is often the ability to mate and reproduce, which is the case between wolves and coyotes. However, from one genus to another the different genetic structures makes it impossible for, say, dogs to mate with cats.

Evolution states that the species developed gradually from lower to higher by means of genetic adaptation. But Genesis 1:11 says that God made the plants and trees "each according to its kind." This distinction pertains explicitly to reproduction: the plants yield "seed according to their kinds" (Genesis 1:12). A tomato plant yields tomato seeds, which sprouts tomato plants. H. C. Leupold comments: "Nature itself here is seen to have definite limits fixed which appear as constant laws or as insurmountable barriers."[104]

In a non-technical sense, the term "evolution" is often used to describe how species adapt to their environments. This is sometimes called "micro-evolution" and poses no conflict to Scripture. There is no doubt that creatures experience variation within their genus and species by means of natural selection. But in its proper sense, "evolution" means the creation of new and *different* kinds of organisms that emerge by natural selection. This is sometimes called "macro-evolution." It is this that the Bible denies in its teaching that God created the various kinds of plants and animals. Thousands of years of careful breeding—not random mutations but intentional genetic manipulation—have produced the wide variety of dogs that we enjoy today. There are considerable differences between a Chihuahua and a Great Dane, showing that there can be changes and variations within a species. But all of this intentional genetic intervention with dogs—not random selection but careful breeding—has never produced anything but a *dog*! The reason is given by Genesis

1, which says that God made the kinds to reproduce within the boundaries he has fixed.

In contrast to the chaos and flux anticipated by evolution, the divine pattern of creation reflects the order and consistency that flows from God's character. Evolutionary science is frustrated by its inability to find proof of natural selection resulting in new kinds of species.[105] It would do better by replacing naturalistic presuppositions with the account of our origins provided by the Creator himself in Genesis 1.

Evolution's Effect on Christianity

Christians should reject evolution because it is not proven and, more importantly, because the testimony of Scripture stands squarely against it. Moreover, we should realize that evolution logically requires the radical revision of essential Christian doctrines. Peter Enns, an Old Testament scholar and evolution advocate, is honest to admit that "evolution cannot simply be grafted onto evangelical Christian faith as an add-on." [106] Rather, to accept the claims of evolution requires the recasting of our entire belief system.

The first topic that requires revision under evolution is the doctrine of *Scripture*. We have observed the fundamental contradiction between the biblical account of creation and the evolutionary account of origins. Because of this clear conflict, Christian proponents of evolution must subordinate the authority of God's Word to secularist dogma and scientific theory, the result of which is the undermining of the Bible's teaching as a whole.

A second casualty of evolution must be the biblical doctrine of *man*. Under evolution, man's unique standing as God's special image-bearer is shaken: he is not above the animals, but rather is one of them. For Christians to embrace evolution would thus be a singular disaster in a culture where the emptiness of secularism has ravaged people with despair and self-loathing. To tell people that they are slightly higher versions of apes is to direct them to a bestial approach to life.

Moreover, the teaching of Adam and Eve as our first created parents is the basis for the unity of the human race and the brotherhood of mankind. Evolution describes our fellow men and women as competitors, so that our hopes for survival require the violent subjugation of those who might threaten our DNA. Evolution is thus a theory compatible with racism. We are but many strands of humanity, some higher and some lower, so that the weak may be dominated by the strong for the evolutionary good of mankind. The value of human life lies only in its utility, rather than man's unique standing as image-bearers of God. Therefore, deformed or weak babies may be justly eliminated and the aged and infirmed may be put to an early end. Under evolution, the value of human life is based on the quality of the genes it passes on and its perceived utility to the world. It is a theory that has already produced the very barbarism that ravaged the twentieth century and is increasingly evident in today's post-Christian society.

Under evolution, the Bible's teaching on *sin* must be replaced. No longer is sin traced to the historical event of the Fall in Genesis 3. Instead, evolution points to defects in man's primitive state which are being corrected by natural selection. Christians thus must renounce the Bible's analysis for the problem of the world, replacing the grand narrative of creation, fall, and redemption with the secularist religion of evolutionary progress. Many pro-evolution Christians will object, insisting that they believe the Bible's teaching on sin. The problem is that they no longer accept the biblical basis for the doctrine of sin, namely, the historical reality of Adam and Eve, their fall into depravity through disobedience, and God's response in justly casting them from paradise.

Along with the abandonment of sin, evolution requires its believers to recast their attitude towards *death*. The Bible ascribes the entry of death to God's judgement on sin (Romans 5:12). Under evolution, mankind ended up as the species it is because death eliminated more inferior alternatives via natural selection. If one still believes in God after embracing evolution, he is a God who wields death as a chief means of bringing about what the Bible describes as creation. When God said, "And it was good" in Genesis 1, he was thus describing a process governed by death and in which death is central to what God approves. This of course calls into question the very goodness of God, so that the mythical image of the Grim Reaper must now be considered one of his primary metaphors. It is hard to imagine a doctrine more offensive to the theology of the Bible than evolution. Under evolution, Christians must abandon in principle our position as people of life and join the secularist culture with its callous embrace of the fundamental necessity and virtue of death.

As an extension of evolution's swath through biblical doctrine, Christian *salvation* must be wholly reorganized. The Christian doctrine of salvation is that the second Adam, Jesus

Christ, has overcome the failure of the first Adam by his life of perfect righteousness and sin-atoning death. Paul summarized: "For as by a man came death, by a man has come also the resurrection of the dead. For as in Adam all die, so also in Christ shall all be made alive" (1 Corinthians 15:21–22). But under evolution, this gospel addresses a sin problem that is mythical, not historically real. If creation and fall are myths, then the Christian gospel cannot escape that same assessment.

The theory of evolution thus assaults the person and work of *Christ*. What does it mean that Jesus was true and perfect man, able on this basis to make an atoning sacrifice for sin? Under evolution, Jesus was an inferior past member of our race, upon whom we now look down from our superior evolutionary perch. Moreover, if Jesus was just one of the many disconnected branches of *homo sapiens*, he could not have taken up our own flesh as kinsman redeemer. Just as the person of Christ is diminished under evolution, his saving work is rendered incomprehensible. The doctrines of penal substitutionary atonement and imputed righteousness find their origin in Genesis 3:21, which evolution can only consider metaphorical at best. Having rejected the historical basis for creation and sin, those who embrace evolution find themselves with no historical relevance for either the life or death of Jesus Christ.

Finally, evolution requires the eventual overthrow of Christian *ethics*. Peter Enns has written: "Some characteristics that Christians have thought of as sinful are understood in an evolutionary scheme as means of ensuring survival—for example, in an evolutionary scheme the aggression and dominance associated with 'survival of the fittest' and sexual promiscuity to perpetuate one's gene pool should be understood as means of ensuring survival."[107] Enns' candor about a needed reappraisal of ethics is valuable. Evolution indeed cannot be grafted onto the structure of biblical Christianity but replaces it with a different structure, a different story of salvation, a different ethic, and a different religion altogether.

Evolution: Small Gain and Great Loss

Given this price tag, we may rightly wonder why any Christian would be attracted to the secularist dogma of evolution. Not only is its scientific basis unproven, but its conflict with Bible teaching and the entirety of Christian doctrine is obvious. The answer is that by at least tolerating evolution, Christians may dramatically tone down our conflict with the secular culture. No longer would Christians have to be considered a cult of obscurantists who refuse to accept what everyone else knows. No longer would our scholars be categorically excluded from the market square of secular academia. No longer would we argue about matters that seem far removed from the good news of forgiveness. With the credibility gained by our tolerance toward evolution, we would gain an opportunity to bear testimony to Jesus as the loving Savior.

Do we realize the folly of this reasoning? Let us consider that it may be true that by embracing evolution we may gain an opportunity to bear witness to Jesus Christ. But to do this we must revert to the very biblical narrative, beginning in Genesis 1–3, which we abandoned in embracing evolution! By the folly of seeking to escape the stigma of a world that does not tolerate God's Word we will have ourselves abandoned the history taught in the Bible, which alone can support the story of the Christian message, the gospel of Jesus as the Savior for our sins.

How little is the gain and how catastrophic must be the loss to a Christianity that capitulates to a narrative designed to replace the teaching of God's Word. But what is the alternative, asks the anguished evangelical, facing the world's demand that we conform or be excluded from society? The biblical alternative was given by Paul: "Let God be true though every one were a liar" (Romans 3:4). We must decide that the Bible is God's Word and therefore the highest authority on every matter to which it speaks. We must be faithful to God by remaining steadfast to his Word. But how can we expect to reach and redeem a world if our teaching results in such an offense that we are deemed a cult of intellectual outrages unwilling to face modern science? We do it in the same way that the apostles and the Christians of the early church did, by the sovereign power of God at work to save through his gospel.

Can Christianity prevail in the face of scientific opposition and cultural ridicule? The Bible answers with its message of a supernatural God of grace, whose redeeming power overcomes sin through the achievement of his Son, Jesus. But how will Christianity go forward and how will the church prevail through history? This question, raised in the Bible's first book is answered by its last book, in Revelation 12:11: "they have conquered ... by the blood of the Lamb and by the word of their testimony, for they loved not their lives even unto death" (Revelation 12:11).

9   *Lights in the Heavens*

Genesis 1:14–19

And God said, "Let there be lights in the expanse of the heavens to separate the day from the night. And let them be for signs and for seasons, and for days and years" (Genesis 1:14).

SOON AFTER MEETING WITH GOD AT THE BURNING BUSH AND receiving his call to Egypt, Moses found himself standing in the presence of mighty Pharaoh. Not only was this a daunting assignment because of the earthly power of Egypt's ruler, but Pharaoh was also held to be the son of the Sun God, Re. Moses understood this, but he stood before Pharaoh as the servant of a far greater God, the Creator of the heavens and the earth. Knowing this, he said: "Thus says the LORD, the God of Israel, 'Let my people go'" (Exodus 5:1). Pharaoh was not impressed. He asked, "Who is the LORD, that I should obey his voice and let Israel go? I do not know the LORD, and moreover, I will not let Israel go" (Exodus 5:2). Moses was undaunted because he knew that the name of the LORD, *Yahweh*, meant, "I Am that I Am" (Exodus 3:14). The God he trusted was the eternal God, the only true God. And through the plagues that followed, Moses attacked and exposed the false gods of Egypt. The ninth plague, the last before the final crushing plague on the firstborn, assailed the supposed realm of Pharaoh's personal God, the sun. Moses stretched out his hand toward heaven and there was "darkness over the land of Egypt," with no light for three days (Exodus 10:22–23). In this way, the supremacy of the true God, the God of Israel, was exerted over the false gods of the Nile so that Pharaoh let God's people go.

Not long after these events, Moses wrote the first chapter of Genesis by the inspiration of God, perhaps while he met with the Lord atop Mount Sinai (see Exodus 34:31–35). The creation account, no less than the plagues that fell on Egypt, involves a put-down of the false gods of the ancient world. This anti-idolatry polemic is especially strong on the fourth day of creation, when "God made the two great lights—the greater light to rule the day and the lesser light to rule the night—and the stars" (Genesis 1:16).

The Fourth Day

The first three creation days were spent constructing the heavens and the earth, making it a fitting inhabitance for God's creatures. Starting with the fourth day, we transition to the second half of the creation week. Here, God creates the beings who will live on the earth. Before making the creatures, however, God placed lights in the heavens: "And God said, 'Let there be lights in the expanse of the heavens to separate the day from the night. And let them be for signs and for seasons, and for days and years, and let them be lights in the expanse of the heavens to give light upon the earth'" (Genesis 1:14–15).

A great deal of the scholarly interest given to these verses concerns how there could be light on the first day of creation when the sun, moon and stars were not made until the fourth day. Moreover, a literal view of Genesis 1 has the plants growing prior to the sun shining. One popular approach is to say that the sun existed on day one but only appeared visibly on day four. The language of verses 14 and 16, however, makes it clear that God created the sun and moon on the fourth day, using the formula, "Let there be," and saying that God "made" them at this time. The problem is solved not by changing the text but by taking it at face value, supposing that God supernaturally provided his own light while the work of creation was proceeding. Then, on the fourth day, God hung the earth's main lights in the sky: the sun by day and the moon by night.

Three tasks are appointed to these luminaries. The first was "to separate the day from the night" (Genesis 1:14). This refers to the way the rising and setting of the sun, together with the appearing of the moon, marks the passage from day to night. It is not the sun that creates the day—God created the day and the night—but the sun's movements regulate daytime and nighttime so long as creation stands.

Second, the lights in the heavens are placed as "signs and for seasons, and for days and years" (Genesis 1:14). God was preparing for the coming of animals and mankind, for whose sake the regular movements of the stars are a means of calculating time and events. By saying that the lights are "for signs," we think of the navigational value of the stars and the use of astral and lunar events for predicting weather. Later in the Bible, God will use eclipses and bright stars to signify great events, such as the birth of Jesus Christ (Joel 2:30; Matthew 2:2). The movements of heavenly bodies exert a great influence on agriculture and nature, including the breeding times of animals and the migration schedules of birds. The stars also provided the basis for calendars, the measuring of "days and years," which in the ancient world could be extraordinarily accurate. Verse 17 states that God "set them in the expanse of the heavens," not randomly but according to his purpose. G. C. Aalders writes that the stars "did not accidentally fall into their designated positions. The whole system was effectively established by God with a view to controlling the orderly rotation of days and nights, years and seasons."[108]

The third assignment given to the heavenly objects was "to give light upon the earth" (Genesis 1:15). The Hebrew word for "lights" is usually applied to "lamps" that reflect the light. The idea here is that even active light sources like the sun are in fact shining a light onto the earth that God has given them. In his goodness towards his creation, God poured out their light which is so beneficial to the growth and well-being of his creatures. We see in the purity of light a reflection of God's own character: 1 John 1:5 says, "God is light, and in him is no darkness at all."

It is remarkable to us that in addition to creating the sun and moon, Genesis off-handedly adds that God made "the stars" (Genesis 1:16). In the ancient world where a cloudless night sky was not washed by street lights, people looked up to a myriad of bright stars in a fantastic array. Today, the night sky the ancients saw is seldom seen except out at sea or in the deep desert. There, the stars are almost overwhelming in their mysterious twinkling over the earth. When Moses casually added to the creation of the fourth day, "and the stars," his first readers were given a sense of the awesome power and sublime wisdom of the God who, as Psalm 147:4 says, "determines the number of the stars; he gives to all of them their names."

Today, we have the advantage of powerful telescopes that present even more fantastic visions of distant stars and galaxies. Together with its vast scope and glorious scenes, the order and design of the universe compel our awareness of the almighty Creator. Johannes Kepler, the founder of modern astronomy, thus said, "The undevout astronomer is mad."[109] Consider the life-sustaining design of Earth and its solar system. It is the earth's precise twenty-three degree slant that gives us our seasons, when a minute deviation in either direction would make life impossible. It is the precise mass and distance of the moon that keeps our tides from either stagnating the ocean or inundating whole continents. Astronomer Geoffrey Marcy wrote in the Washington Post about the marvel of our solar system, apparently unique in its design to sustain life. "It's like a jewel," he said. "You've got circular orbits. They're all in the same plane … It's perfect, you know. It's gorgeous. It's almost uncanny."[110] Marcy's comments echo those of Isaac Newton 300 years before: "This most beautiful system of the sun, planets, and comets could only proceed from the counsel and dominion of an intelligent and powerful Being."[111]

The Only True God

Just as the spectacular design of the universe rebukes the unbelief of atheistic scientists, Genesis 1 seems to involve an intentional assault against ancient idolatry. We have already noted the awesomeness of the starry sky, so it is not surprising that people who were bound in sin would begin to worship heavenly objects like the sun and moon. Moses therefore warns his readers against worshiping heavenly objects, since they are still things made by the true God.

This polemic against idolatry began in verse 1, where "In the beginning, God created the heavens and the earth." Unlike the pagan conception of limited gods who indwelt nature, and in many cases were merely local to a specific territory or people, the God of the Bible is eternal and transcendent. He created the entirety of the universe.

But it is especially when Genesis 1 turns to the sun, moon, and stars that it targets the objects of false, idolatrous worship. Gordon Wenham explains: "In neighboring cultures, the sun and the moon were some of the most important gods in the pantheon, and the stars were often credited with controlling human destiny."[112] These heavenly objects often had their own religious cults, mythologies, priests, and devotees. But Genesis 1 says, "No, these are not gods!" They are created lamps to shine God's light on the earth and perform the functions the Creator has assigned them. This is a point that would be made throughout the Old Testament. Isaiah wrote that the stars urge us to worship only the Lord, relying on his wisdom and might: "Lift up your eyes on high and see: who created these? He who brings out their host by number, calling them all by name" (Isaiah 40:26). If God created and determines the function of the heavenly lights, we would be fools to worship them or consult the stars for our fate.

This treatment of the sun and moon shows how unwilling Moses was to suggest even a hint of the mythological pantheon common to the pagan nations. It is probably significant that Genesis 1:16 does not name them. Instead,

Moses calls the sun and moon "the two great lights—the greater light to rule the day and the lesser light to rule the night." The Hebrew words for sun and moon, *shemesh* and *yareach*, were used in other Semitic languages as names of high deities. So Genesis 1 will not personalize their creation by using these names when they are in reality mere objects under God's control. Similarly, the almost dismissive manner in which Moses says "also the stars" may well be a way of putting the idolatrous myths in their place. John Currid makes clear the message from creation's fourth day: "Luminaries are mere material objects with no life of their own, and they are never to be worshiped" (see Deuteronomy 4:19).[113]

In contrast, David Atkinson notes how God's creation of the stars should humble us before him in reverent awe: "The majesty and mystery of God, seen 'through his works', was surely part of the faith of the author of Genesis 1. He would no doubt have concurred with the psalmist: 'When I look at thy heavens, the work of thy fingers, the moon and the stars which thou hast established; what is man that thou art mindful of him' (Psalm 8:3–4)."[114] The ancient poet who penned Psalm 136 certainly took this view. In response to the created heavenly lights, he exclaimed:

Give thanks to the LORD, for he is good,
for his steadfast love endures forever ...
to him who made the great lights,
for his steadfast love endures forever;
the sun to rule over the day,
for his steadfast love endures forever;
the moon and stars to rule over the night,
for his steadfast love endures forever (Psalm 136:1, 7–9).

Like Stars in the Sky

When we studied Genesis 1:2, we noted that by describing the original, unformed mass of creation as desolate and uninhabited, God was anticipating his future intention. The first of those concerns was answered in days one to three of creation as God made the once-desolate creation into a lush and watered world. The second intention is solved when God inhabits the earth with creatures.

We look on the fourth day of creation and see the heavenly lights that God placed into the expanse of the heavens. If we look forward in Scripture and ask how God later uses this imagery and language, the result is staggering. I say this because the imagery of the fourth day with its shining stars in the dark sky is applied consistently in Scripture to *us*, the people of God who are redeemed through his covenant of grace. When Abraham complained about his lack of offspring, God took him out under the night sky and had him look upwards: "'Look toward heaven, and number the stars, if you are able to number them.' Then he said to him, 'So shall your offspring be'" (Genesis 15:5). The New Testament assures us that this refers to Abraham's spiritual offspring, that is, those who join him through faith in the saving promises of God (Galatians 3:7). The contemporary Christian singer Rich Mullins put it well: "Sometimes I think of Abraham, how one star he saw had been lit for me."[115]

If we think that God's point to Abraham involved merely the number of the stars rather than the stars themselves, Jesus' later teaching clarifies. At the end of his parable of the sower, Jesus noted that history will end with a great separation. When he returns with his angels, he will gather all who remain in their sin through unbelief for the fiery furnace of eternal condemnation. Those who were cleansed by his blood and renewed by his Spirit remained. Jesus then stated: "Then the righteous will shine like the sun in the kingdom of their Father" (Matthew 13:43). Daniel 12:3 applied this same imagery to faithful believers: "those who are wise shall shine like the brightness of the sky above; and those who turn many to righteousness, like the stars forever and ever."

Given the Bible's own use of this imagery to describe believers, I would note that the assignments God gave to the heavenly lights provide a convenient summary of the believers' calling in following Christ. First, God put the lights in the heavens "to separate the day from the night" (Genesis 1:14). In like manner, God intends for us to distinguish clearly between faith and unbelief. There is the church and the world, holiness and sin, truth and error. We noted in our study of the third day that God created the world with clear distinctions and he separated things that should not be confused. Likewise, Christians are to distinguish correctly, following carefully the path laid out in God's Word.

The great need of our generation is Christians who know how to live *in* the world but not *of* the world, who know how to separate light from darkness. Paul made this very point to the believers in Philippi, urging them to live carefully according to the light of God: "Do all things without grumbling or questioning, that you may be blameless and innocent, children of God without blemish in the midst of a crooked and twisted generation, among whom you shine as lights in the world, holding fast to the word of life" (Philippians 2:14–16). To the Ephesians, Paul likewise called for holiness of life as Christians separated themselves, refusing to become partners with those committed to sin: "for at one time you were darkness, but now you are light in the Lord. Walk as children of light" (Ephesians 5:8).

Second, God created the heavenly lights to serve as signs for those living on the earth. A sign points to something or someone else. Christians are to be signs for others to see the grace and power of Jesus Christ in salvation. Jesus said in Revelation 22:16, "I am ... the bright Morning Star." He is now equipping us to bear testimony to his glory and grace before the world. He told us to hold fast, conquer by faith, and keep his works until the end (Revelation 2:25–26), and promised to each one: "I will give him the morning star" (Revelation 2:28). If you hold fast, live by faith, and pursue his works, Jesus will make you a lamp in which his own shining light will be seen.

Third, God made the heavenly lights "to give light upon the earth" (Genesis 1:15). In addition to our witness, Jesus applied this teaching to our calling to do good works that declare God's glory:

> You are the light of the world. ... let your light shine before others, so that they may see your good works and give glory to your Father who is in heaven (Matthew 5:14–16).

Light illuminates, and we are to shine forth the way of salvation through the gospel of Jesus Christ. Light warms, and we are to extend the love of God in Christ to hurting people in the world. Light exposes, and the gracious, godly lifestyles of believers are to stand in stark contrast with the crude, ungodly pattern of this world. Light guides and directs. We are likewise to offer the wholesome truth of God's Word that our generation so greatly needs to hear.

Fourth, God made the sun and moon "to rule over the day and over the night" (Genesis 1:18). The point was that the sun and moon stand above their respective spheres, dominating the portion of time granted to them by God. This provocative language seems odd when spoken about impersonal objects, however great they are. Perhaps God spoke of the sun and moon ruling with an eye to the influence that Christians and the church are to have over each generation.

Christians rule not by force, compulsion, or pride. We reign with Christ through prayers that go from our hearts to the very throne of heaven above. Christians determine the course of the world by our willingness to stand for Jesus and God's truth against all opposition. It was Christians from England and America in the last two centuries who left the safety of their homes and took the gospel through great peril to darkened lands, often at the cost of their lives, and changed the world. It was a believer like William Wilberforce who stood up before the House of Commons in England and demanded that the slave trade end. It is Christians today who stand up amidst a culture of death and plead for the dignity and value of every human life, whether born or unborn. It is the Christian in the classroom, in the workplace, in the family, or in the neighborhood, who offers hope of salvation through the gospel witness only he or she can provide.

In Revelation 5:10, the watching spirits in heaven give praise to Christ on behalf of his faithful, suffering, light-bearing church on earth, saying: "you have made them a kingdom and priests to our God, and they shall reign on the earth." Do we realize that what we do as a church and as Christians is always the single most significant earthly factor in our culture and generation? If we do not courageously proclaim God's truth from his Word, how will the world ever hear it? If we do not invite unbelieving friends to the salvation Jesus alone can give, how can they ever be redeemed?

Do we fear the world and its power too much to play the role God has assigned to us? Then let's remember Moses standing before mighty Pharaoh and the gods of the Nile. The God who sends us today as lights in the world is the same God who delivered Moses and broke the false idols of that generation. He created the sun, moon, and stars and apportioned their tasks in the dawn of creation. May we, too, by faith in his great power, be faithful to shine the holy light so needed in our world today.

10   *The Living Creatures*

Genesis 1:20–26

Then God said, "Let us make man in our image, after our likeness. And let them have dominion over the fish of the sea and over the birds of the heavens and over the livestock and over all the earth and over every creeping thing that creeps on the earth" (Genesis 1:26).

IN HIS BOOK, *PALE BLUE DOT*, CARL SAGAN DESCRIBES AN IMAGE of Earth taken by the *Voyager* spacecraft from billions of miles away. In it, our planet is a tiny point of light amidst the vast field of stars. Sagan urged that the picture should persuade us of our insignificance to the cosmos: "Our posturing, our imagined self-importance, the delusion that we have some privileged position in the universe, are challenged by this point of pale light."[116] Genesis 1, despite its brevity of description, does nothing to dispel the grandeur of the universe. Yet it draws exactly the opposite conclusion regarding the human race. We earlier noted that the Bible's creation account is remarkably earth-centered.[117] As we draw near to the end of the creation week we may say more specifically that Genesis 1 is remarkably man-centered. The great actor in this chapter is of course God the Creator. But, as John Calvin observed, "God made everything with man in mind."[118]

According to Genesis 1, in all the great universe that God has made, there is no more significant being outside himself than the human being. After all, everything made up to this point has an ultimate purpose aimed at mankind. God made a planet with a breathable atmosphere, with plenteous water and land. God then made plant life to serve as food and set the lights in the sky as clocks and calendars. On the fifth and sixth days, God created fish, birds, and beasts. Then, at the climax of creation, "God said, 'Let us make man in our image, after our likeness'" (Genesis 1:26). James Boice comments that man "is the peak of creation. Moreover, from this point on the story of Genesis is the story of man—in rebellion against God but also as the object of His special love and redemption."[119]

The Fifth Day

Before the coming of man, however, God gave his attention to creating the animals. On the fifth day, God created the sea animals who swim in the waters and the birds who arch their flight across the heavens. These creatures correspond to the spaces prepared earlier on the second day, the sea and the sky (Genesis 1:6–8). The significance of these creatures is seen in the use—only for the second time in Genesis 1—of the word "created" (Hebrew, *bara*): "So God created the great sea creatures and every living creature that moves, with which the waters swarm, according to their kinds, and every winged bird according to its kind" (Genesis 1:21).

The first use of the word "create" was in Genesis 1:1, where God "created the heavens and the earth." Then, we noted that it is used only of God and involves *creation ex nihilo*: making something that had no prior existence. What is new here is the appearance of the "living creatures" (Genesis 1:20). The word for "living" is the Hebrew word *nephesh*, which means "soul." In distinction from the unthinking plant-world, these sea and air creatures, soon to be joined by the beasts of the ground, have an inner awareness and will. By creating these "living creatures" the Creator displayed himself as a living God who possesses infinite power and genius.

The first category of living creatures are those that dwell in the sea: "God said, 'Let the waters swarm with swarms of living creatures'" (Genesis 1:20). "So God created the great sea creatures and every living creature that moves, with which the waters swarm, according to their kinds" (Genesis 1:21). When verse 20 speaks of the waters "swarming" with living creatures, it speaks to the incredible variety of creatures that inhabit the seas and sprang forth at God's command.

Verse 21 emphasizes the "great sea creatures" (Hebrew, *tanninim*), a word that can be used for various large sea animals, including snakes (Exodus 7:12), great serpents (Deuteronomy 32:33) and dragons (Ezekiel 29:3). Often, it is translated as "monsters" (Jeremiah 51:34). The idea would include all the large sea creatures, including whales and crocodiles. Scholars have noted that Canaanite creation myths featured a great sea serpent who was the enemy of the chief god and represented the powers of chaos, which are often associated with the sea. If Moses intended such a reference, his point would have been God's sovereignty over the sea and its most dreadful monsters. Gordon Wenham writes: "They are not rivals that have to be defeated, just one of his many creatures."[120] Psalm 148:7 agrees, urging: "Praise the LORD from the earth, you great sea creatures and all deeps."

Along with the swarming fish, God commanded: "and let birds fly above the earth across the expanse of the heavens" (Genesis 1:20). Therefore, "God created ... every winged bird according to its kind" (Genesis 1:21). As with the plants and the fish, the birds were all created in God-designed genuses. Some of the most avid hobbyists are bird-watchers, who engross themselves in the great variety between eagles, owls, robins, and wrens. They also log the wide range of habits when it comes to flight, mating, migrating, and nesting. All of these differences bear testimony to the remarkable diversity in the creative beauty of God's mind. Verse 21 concludes that "God saw that it was good." We might not only agree but raise the pitch to "wonderful," "spectacular," and "awesome"!

The "living creatures" are not only specially created, but they also are the first recipients of God's specific blessing in the creation account: "And God blessed them, saying, 'Be fruitful and multiply and fill the waters in the seas, and let birds multiply on the earth'" (Genesis 1:22). God's blessing indicates God's continuing purpose for his living creatures. God designed a future for them as well as a present. Moreover, God's blessing conveyed with it the power to bring about his designed purpose. In this case, the blessing of God was the fruitfulness of the fish and birds in producing offspring so as to multiply and fill the waters and sky. Inherent to their being is the power of reproduction, so that God's desire was fulfilled as these wonderful creatures spread throughout the earth.

The blessing of God is a theme that will recur throughout Genesis. When God commands his creatures, it is always in light of the blessing he has already given. This holds true for us: whatever God commands us is in light of the enormous blessings we have received. In Genesis, God will bless the animals, mankind, the Sabbath, and then the people called into his covenant. How often this blessing will take the form of children and an abundance of offspring. We live in a time when more than a few married couples are not granted children, so God blesses them in other ways. But the biblical view of life is one that especially values children as precious gifts from God. It is an outlook that speaks not so much of the success that we can attain but the blessing that God is pleased to give.[121]

In Genesis 1:22, the broad principle of God's desire for life is displayed, just as it is repeatedly enacted by the fish and the birds today. The salmon drives itself into the current in order to reach the spawning ground where God's blessing may be fulfilled. John Calvin writes of the zeal of mother birds who look "like they are willing to kill themselves because of the love they have for reproducing their kind." He asks, "Where does all that come from? From the power of that word back when God said, 'Be fruitful and multiply on the earth.'"[122] In this, the lower animals set an example for us in seeking to fulfill God's purposes. Calvin concludes: "Therefore, let us profit from the school of birds, and all other creatures. When we see that they yield themselves captive to God's word, let us individually and with all humility try hard to follow his word, which is not for our confusion but for our instruction so that we will please him by accepting everything he commands."[123]

The Sixth Day

The days of creation show a parallel pattern so that the first and fourth, second and fifth, and third and sixth days are related. The second day prepared the waters below and the sky above to be filled by God's creatures on the fifth day, so also the third day prepared the land, which God filled on the sixth day with living creatures: "And God said, 'Let the earth bring forth living creatures according to their kinds—livestock and creeping things and beasts of the earth according to their kinds.' And it was so" (Genesis 1:24).

God's creation of the animals makes clear that the beasts are part of the planet; they belong in a sense, to the earth: "Let the earth bring forth" (Genesis 1:24). These land animals were created in three categories. First is "livestock." These are domesticated animals such as cattle. Their name (Hebrew, *behemah*) has the root meaning of being "dumb," signifying God intention for them to provide lowly service to mankind. The second category is "creeping things," which would include reptiles, worms, and other beings that crawl on or under the ground. Third is "beasts of the earth," which refers to the wild animals, such as lions and bears. The Hebrew for "beasts" is "living things," signifying the vitality and energy of these remarkable creatures. Even in the peace of the original creation, before death and violence, these wild beasts were designed by God to live free and undomesticated. Within these categories were all the main groups of animals, each "according to their kinds" (Genesis 1:24). They were not the product of random chance or evolution but products of God's personal design and powerful creation.

Genesis 1 does not launch into a taxonomy of the various

species of land beasts. But it certainly invites this kind of study to the glory of God. Indeed, it is through the diversity of the animals, together with fish and birds, and also the staggering complexity of the stars and galactic systems, that God displays a creative imagination that overwhelms our hearts. God not only made these wonderful things and creatures but he built into nature his creative capacity. "Let the waters swarm," he commanded, and "Let the earth bring forth" (Genesis 1:20, 24). David Wilkinson writes: "God builds into the natural world the process of his creativity. Thus the natural world provides an intricate tapestry bearing witness to the creativity of God."[124] Psalm 104:24 exults: "O LORD, how manifold are your works! In wisdom have you made them all; the earth is full of your creatures."

Man and His Dominion

For all the glorious diversity of the sea, air, and land creatures, God was not yet finished filling his earth. There was one last creature to come forth and live, a creature above all the others and designed especially for a personal fellowship with the Creator. Genesis 1:26 reports:

> Then God said, "Let us make man in our image, after our likeness. And let them have dominion over the fish of the sea and over the birds of the heavens and over the livestock and over all the earth and over every creeping thing that creeps on the earth."

Before exploring man's special status in relationship to God, we should note that mankind was made in solidarity with the other "living creatures" of the earth. Man shares this designation with the animals, being referred to in Genesis

2:7 as a "living creature," just as they are. Moreover, while verse 27 employs the third instance of God's special creation (Hebrew, *bara*) in this chapter, marking off man as a new and special being, verse 26 first sees God making him in a manner similar to other living creatures. So while man is categorically different from the fish, birds, and animals, he is like them in significant ways. Like the animals, man is made on the sixth day from the earth (Genesis 1:24, 2:7), he feeds on the same food that they eat (Genesis 1:29–30), and reproduces according to God's blessing just as they do (Genesis 1:22, 28). John Sailhamer thus notes that man "can well be studied partly through the study of [the other living creatures]; they are half his context."[125]

Still, it is mankind's special relationship to God that shapes our identity. We will consider the meaning of the image of God more fully in the next chapter. But, viewing man among the "living creatures," we can note his *supremacy* as the climax of God's creation. Man's high status is seen in God's deliberation prior to his making: "Then God said, 'Let us make man in our image'" (Genesis 1:26).

Who is this "us" to whom God is speaking? Earlier generations of Christians assumed that this was an occasion where the Trinity is seen in the Old Testament: the "us" is the Son and the Spirit together with the Creator Father. Most scholars today doubt this interpretation. Some suggest that God is speaking to the angelic court, as in Isaiah 6:8, where God said to the angels, "Whom shall I send, and who will go for us?" But there is no mention of angels in Genesis 1. Moreover, man is not created in the image of angels, as this view would require (see Psalm 8:5). Perhaps the most popular view today is that God is using the "royal we." He is not addressing another person but speaking of himself in exalted tones. The problem is that this aristocratic tradition is not rooted in the Bible; while the Queen of England may speak of herself, saying, "we," God never does apart from the other members of the Trinity.

This brings us back to the traditional view of God the Father addressing his fellow persons in the Trinity. After all, it is only they together, as "us," who could create in "our" divine image. In Genesis 1:2, we met the Spirit of God hovering over the waters, and the New Testament identifies the Word of God in Genesis 1:3 as God the Son (John 1:1–2). It seems best, then, to see the Creator Father addressing the Creator Spirit and the Creator Son, deliberating on the climactic moment in all creation: the creation of man in their image.

It is by virtue of his special creation in the image of God that man rises above the other living creatures. Bruce Waltke writes; "Whereas the other creatures are created 'according to their kinds' (Genesis 1:21, 24, 25), humanity is made 'in the image of God.'"[126] Do you see the contrast? Waltke contines: "Being made in God's image establishes humanity's role on earth and facilitates communication with the divine."[127] This understanding grounds the special dignity of human beings. Men and women do not claim their special value on the basis of egotistic arrogance but rather by God's design in our creation. It is on this ground that God will later express horror at the taking of human life (Genesis 9:5–6). Because this teaching grounds our human identity in God, Francis Schaeffer wrote that for contemporary mankind "this phrase,

the image of God, is as important as anything in Scripture."
Schaeffer explains:

> In his own naturalistic theories ... with an evolutionary
> concept of a mechanical, chance parade from the atom
> to man, man has lost his unique identity. As he looks out
> upon the world, as he faces the machine, he cannot tell
> himself from what he faces. He cannot distinguish himself
> from other things.[128]

How important it is, then, for the Christian to see his and
her identity as grounded in God and tell the despairing world
that we were made in God's image, with a dignity and value
established by our origin.

In addition to showing mankind's *supremacy* over the
other living creatures, Genesis 1:26 identifies man as God's
representative on earth. To say that man was made in God's
"image" and "likeness" means that man embodies things
about God for the rest of creation to see. Clyde Francisco
writes: "although man is like God, he is not God. Man is not
deity but reflects the divine nature within his humanity."[129]
Realizing mankind's role helps us to understand the logic of
the second commandment, which forbids making images
for the worship of God (Exodus 20:4–5). Man is not to
worship *through* images of God but rather to worship *as* the
image of God. Vinoth Ramachandra writes: "when human
beings fashion images out of the created world and worship
them, they worship something inferior to them and thus
dehumanize themselves."[130]

Ancient idolatry operated on the principle that an image
could not only represent God but also exercised his powers.

Often the king was considered the image of God, as seen in inscriptions from Egypt and Assyria.[131] But it is not a block of stone and not even just the divinized person of the ruler who bears God's image: it is all of mankind—each and every man, woman, and child—who bears God's image in the world. The spirit of this ideal was expressed by Jesus in his Sermon on the Mount: "You are the light of the world. ... Let your light shine before others, so that they may see your good works and give glory to your Father who is in heaven" (Matthew 5:14–16).

Genesis 1:26 further emphasizes the *rule* of mankind over the earth: "let them have dominion over the fish of the sea and over the birds of the heavens and over the livestock and over all the earth and over every creeping thing that creeps on the earth." Mankind is to govern the world and its creatures as stewards on God's behalf. This mandate provides the basis both for man's employment of the earth and man's conservation of the earth. Our rulership of the world must be for the fulfillment of God's purposes and the display of God's glory, rather than our own sinful self-interest. Francis Schaeffer writes: "As that which was created, man is no higher than all that has been created; but as created in the image of God, he has the responsibility to consciously care for all that which God put in his care."[132]

Crowned with Glory and Honor

In Psalm 8, King David wrote a short poetic commentary on Moses' account of man's creation. The psalm begins and ends with praise to God: "O Lord, our Lord, how majestic is your name in all the earth!" (Psalm 8:1, 9). In between, David reflects on the order of the created realm. He notes that God made man "a little lower than the heavenly beings" but also gave "him dominion over the works of [God's] hands; [God has] put all things under his feet, all sheep and oxen, and also the beasts of the field, the birds of the heavens, and the fish of the sea" (Psalm 8:5–8). In other words, David realized that man was created as a mediating being. We stand below God and above the lower creatures. As Genesis 1 teaches, we are made from the earth like the other living creatures but we are made in the image of God.

This observation raises a question that is vitally important in our time. If mankind is made below God and above the animals, in which direction are we to look? Are we to look down and think of ourselves as a slightly superior kind of animal or are we to look up and think of ourselves as the image-bearers of God on earth? The answer is given in David's statement that man was made "a little lower than the heavenly beings and crowned him with glory and honor" (Psalm 8:5). Notice that we are a little lower than God rather than a little higher than beasts. While we mediate between heaven and earth, we are to form our identity in terms of our higher relationship with God. We live in the world according to God's standards and will, and exercise his rule on the earth.

Like Genesis 1, Psalm 8 presents man both in his humility as a creature and in his glory as God's special creation. We are "living creatures" together with the other animals (Genesis 1:26), so we bow in humility before God: "what is man that you are mindful of him, and the son of man that you care for him?" But Psalm 8 also notes that as those who bear the image of God, we are to have our faces and our hearts directed upward to him: in joy, obedience, and worshipful awe of the Creator who made us in his own image.

A later interpretation of Psalm 8, and therefore of Genesis 1:26, is Hebrews 2:6–9, which not only quotes Psalm 8 but takes notice of how much our dominion has gone awry. Our problem is: "At present, we do not yet see everything in subjection to him," that is, the human race (Hebrews 2:8). What an understatement! We do not have things under control! Our sin has made a ruin not only of the world but of our own lives, alienating us from God and placing us under his wrath. Hebrews, however, adds the solution: "But we see him who for a little while was made lower than the angels, namely Jesus, crowned with glory and honor because of the suffering of death ... by the grace of God" (Hebrews 2:9).

Perhaps the reason so many people refuse to look upward today, but seek their identity with the animals and a lower way of life, is that they realize how our sin has failed God and earned his displeasure. The answer is Jesus Christ. Trusting him, we may look up to God again, having been forgiven of our sins through his death. We can humbly embrace our biblical status above the creatures and bear God's image without falling into arrogance or pride. Jesus is God the Son who became man that he might restore God's image in mankind.

The God who created all things and created man to bear his image does not intend to fail in his purpose. Jesus came and exercised a triumphant dominion, overcoming the guilt and power of sin through his conquering atonement on the cross. Now, enthroned in an eternal and universal dominion, incarnate as both God and man, and "crowned with glory and

honor because of the suffering of [his] death" (Hebrews 2:9),
Jesus can restore us to God and our original calling. Through
faith in Jesus, we will be placed not only on our high perch
of dominion above the creatures, but according to God's
Word we will be enthroned with Christ in God's presence,
bearing God's glorious image and praising God's wonderful
name not only on earth but in heaven forever. If we will trust
in him whom God has sent for us, God will crown us again
with "glory and honor" (Psalm 8:5). Jesus promises to those
who call on his name: "I will give you the crown of life"
(Revelation 2:10).

I I   *In the Image of God*

Genesis 1:26–27

So God created man in his own image, in the image of God he created him; male and female he created them (Genesis 1:27).

IF YOU WANT TO UNDERSTAND SOMETHING, ONE OF THE BEST things to do is study its origin or founding. This is true of nations. If you want to understand why America is as it is today, what its institutions are about and how its self-identity formed, then you have to go back and learn about its birth in the Revolutionary War, its struggle as a colony seeking independence, its ideal of equality under God, and its desire for life, liberty, and the pursuit of happiness.

The same is true of sports and pastimes. I recently investigated the invention of the great American sport of football. American football has its roots in the English game of rugby. In the 1880s Walter Camp, captain of the Yale University team, introduced rule changes that transformed the sport to what we know today. He began the line of scrimmage, the point differential between touchdowns and field goals, and the eleven-man limit on the field. In 1906, when the game was bogging down in mass brutality, he innovated the forward pass. In all of these transformations Camp was seeking to take the British virtues of physical strength and stamina and add the American ethos of speed, daring, and strategy. These are the very things that explain the vital connection between American football and the American spirit.

If you want to understand man, including yourself as a human being, it will also be important to consider your origin. You of course need to know your parents and place of birth, and it is only natural for people to be interested in their more distant ancestry. But the most important ancestors for you to know about are your first set of parents and their origin. Genesis 1:27 provides this vital information: "God created man in his own image." It is this origin that gives you a special value. R. Kent Hughes states that if you "could travel a hundred times the speed of light, past countless yellow-orange stars, to the edge of the galaxy and swoop down to the fiery glow located a few hundred light-years below the plane of the Milky Way," and if you "could witness a star's birth, in all your stellar journeys you would never see anything equal to the birth and wonder of a human being."[133] That baby human rests at the very pinnacle of creation, for it is made in the image of God! "He or she will exist forever. When the stars of the universe fade away, that soul shall still live."[134]

The Image and Likeness of God

Despite the great significance of the statement that "God created man in his own image," the meaning of these words has been hard to nail down. What is clear is that "image" and "likeness" speak of resemblance. The word for "image" (Hebrew, *tselem*) has the meaning of something that is carved or cut out. "After our likeness" (Genesis 1:26) makes much the same point, defining man as like God though not himself divine. John Calvin defines the *imago dei* by saying that "man resembles him and that in him God's glory is contemplated, as in a mirror."[135] The same language is used in Genesis 5:3 when Adam has a son: "he fathered a son in his own likeness, after his image." Alasdair Paine writes: "Seth is a chip off the old block. Being in God's image means being a chip off his."[136]

While it is not difficult to understand what it means to bear God's image, the question that is difficult is *how* man bears God's image. *What* is it about mankind that bears analogy to God?

One historic answer is that man bears God's image by virtue of the nobility of our physical form. Man walks upright among the beasts, as God's royal delegate on earth. The problem with this view is that God does not possess a body, since "God is spirit" (John 4:24). So it is not likely that we represent him primarily through our physical form.

With our inner faculties in view, the most common way to define the image of God is through aspects of the human nature that elevate us above the animals. Augustine proposed that the image of God resides in man's memory, understanding and will, seeking in this way to mirror God's Trinitarian personhood.[137] Others point to man's self-awareness and personality, which are of a higher order than animals. The English preacher and poet John Donne wrote: "the difference between the reason of man and the instinct of the beast is this, that the beast does but know, but the man knows that he knows."[138] Man further possesses a sense of conscience and performs moral decision-making. Man does not live by mere instinct like the animals, but with a divinely imprinted moral compass designed to glorify and obey God's law.

Moreover, man alone worships God with spiritual awareness. Solomon wrote that God "has put eternity into man's heart" (Ecclesiastes 3:11). Only man is aware of a world beyond his senses. However intelligent and loyal an animal may seem, it remains a creature of the earth, from which it came (Genesis 1:24). Man alone faces death with an awareness of the afterlife and with a sense of meeting God beyond the grave. With man's ability to know and worship God comes the responsibility to fulfill our chief end as God's beloved creatures: "to glorify God and enjoy him forever."

The Image as a Community of Love

After saying that God made man in his own image, Genesis 1:27 makes a significant addition: "male and female he created them." This statement grounds the fundamental equality between the sexes. People often blame the Bible for repressing women, but the opposite is actually the case. It is hard to imagine a more radical social comment in Moses' second-millennium context than to grant the image of God to women. It is remarkable enough that Genesis says that God made *all* humans in his image, not merely human rulers. But to say that God made *women* as well as men in his own image may have been the single most elevating comment ever uttered regarding the female sex.

The Bible will go on to note differences between males and females. Men are called to covenant headship throughout the Bible, both in the church (1 Timothy 2:11) and in the home (Ephesians 5:25). Women bear the high calling of being helpers to men (Genesis 2:18). But we should never think that this complementarian arrangement results from inferiority on the part of women. Men and women equally bear the image of God and are of equal dignity and value before him.

As well as grounding the equality of men and women, Genesis 1:27 declares the distinctiveness of male and female, and also sexuality as the gift of God the Creator. Victor Hamilton writes: "Sexuality is not an accident of nature, nor is it simply a biological phenomenon. Instead it is a gift of God."[139]

In an age of such incredible confusion that gender is declared a social construct or personal choice—this in the face of irrefutable biological determinism—the Bible declares sexual identity to be created by God. If you are male, it is because maleness is intrinsic to your God-designed being. If you are a woman, it was God who made you female at the moment you came into existence. A man may deny his gender, put on a dress or even take hormone treatments to violate himself chemically. But he will never be a woman, or vice versa. Not only does the Bible declare the sexual difference but it sets men and women on distinctive, though complementary, paths. As Kenneth Matthews writes: "The proper role of the sexes ... is crucial to God's designs for human life and prosperity."[140] Since our sexual identity is created by God, it should be honored through a grateful pursuit of his design.

One reason for the emphasis given to mankind's male and female identities seems to be that bearing the image of God involves living in loving community. God himself exists within loving community—as Father, Son, and Spirit experience eternal and perfect love—so mankind bears God's image in relationships of community and love.

We see this theme in Genesis 2, where the pinnacle of creation is not merely man as male and female but man as husband and wife. Realizing this suggests that we bear God's image through our capacity to love one another, especially in covenant union, in a way that reflects the holy and giving love within God. In this way, the Bible's beginning connects seamlessly with the Bible's end, where history concludes with Christ as the groom taking the church as his bride in a love relationship that will never end. John wrote, "God is love" (1 John 4:8). Therefore, men and women bear God's image most significantly when we share his love with one another. John said: "Beloved, let us love one another, for love is from God, and whoever loves has been born of God and knows God" (1 John 4:7).

The Image as Communion with God

So far, we have considered the image of God mainly in terms of the inner life of the human nature. Mankind was made with personality, morality, and spirituality. We expanded our thought to include the idea that men and women bear God's image in relationships of love. In recent years, however, scholars have emphasized that the image of God in man involves our creation for a relationship with himself. In the highest sense, man in the image of God speaks of our identity in communion with the Creator.

Knowing God is intrinsic to man's creation in God's image. The animals are unaware of God. They do not seek or worship their Maker. But mankind, Paul says, knows God because he has designed creation to reveal himself to his image-bearers (Romans 1:19). So vital is this aspect of our humanity that Jesus exclaimed: "now this is eternal life, that they know you, the only true God" (John 17:3).

The biblical idea of knowledge involves more than possessing information. It involves communion and fellowship. We see this in the contrasting way that God began dealing with mankind versus his dealing with the animals. In Genesis 1:22, God pronounces his blessing on the fish and birds: "God blessed them, saying, 'Be fruitful and multiply.'" The same blessing is granted to mankind but with a crucial difference. Genesis 1:28 says: "And God blessed them. And God said to them, 'Be fruitful and multiply.'" The difference is seen in the added words, "And God said to them." God put his blessing on the fish and birds, but God blessed man by means of personal communication designed to foster a relationship of faith and love.

Together with our relationship with God, bearing God's image involves our becoming like him. Paul says in Ephesians 4:24 that believers have been "created after the likeness of God in true righteousness and holiness." So in addition to the knowledge of God, the image of God involves a right standing with God and holiness before him. The point of this righteousness and holiness, like our knowledge of God, is for the sake of an eternal communion in love with our Maker. With this in mind the *Westminster Confession of Faith* gives its definition of the *imago dei*: "God … created man, male and female, with reasonable and immortal souls, endued with knowledge, righteousness, and true holiness, after His own image".[141]

Genesis 2:7 tells us of how God made Adam: "The LORD God formed the man of dust from the ground and breathed into his nostrils the breath of life." God made man face-to-face for a covenantal relationship of fellowship, communion, and love. This, too, is seen at the end of the Bible just as here in the beginning. As heirs together with Jesus Christ, Christians enter into an inheritance that consists of God's gift of himself. Revelation 21:3 says: "He will dwell with them, and they will be his people, and God himself will be with them as their God." Revelation 22:4–5 goes further, using imagery taken straight out of Genesis 1: "They will see his face, and his name will be on their foreheads … the Lord God will be their light, and they will reign forever and ever."

Let's connect the image of God to our pursuit of a Christian worldview in Genesis 1. Genesis 1:1 tells us *where* we are living: in a world created by a transcendent, holy, and almighty God, a world with purpose and history under the Creator's sovereign will. Genesis 1:27 reveals *what* I am: a living creature made by God to bear his own image. The stamp of God is seen in our souls, which possess moral and spiritual self-awareness. Above all, we are creatures designed by God to know God, for spiritual communion with our Maker in knowledge and righteousness. What could grant a greater dignity—along with humility—before God, together with a high sense of calling and privilege! We are creatures designed to know and be known by God, and to love and be loved by the Creator himself!

The Image of God Fallen & Restored

There is a problem, however: the image of God in man has

been shattered by sin. Genesis 3 ends, after the breaking of God's covenant, with these words: God "drove out the man, and at the east of the garden of Eden he placed the cherubim and a flaming sword ... to guard the way to the tree of life" (Genesis 3:24). Man, made as royalty amidst the creatures, became a servant to the earth: "the LORD God sent him out from the garden of Eden to work the ground from which he was taken" (Genesis 3:23).

Two questions are raised by man's fall into sin. The first question is whether the image of God was lost to fallen mankind. The answer is both No and Yes. First, the Bible indicates that fallen man retains the image of God with respect to our value and dignity. We see this truth when God forbids the taking of human life. He told Noah, long after the fall: "Whoever sheds the blood of man, by man shall his blood be shed, for God made man in his own image" (Genesis 9:6). The sanctity of human life continues under sin, since man was made in the image of God.

On the other hand, man has lost the vital core of the divine image, in the form of righteousness and holiness in relating to God. The result of sin, therefore, has been not the complete loss of the divine image but rather its thorough corruption. Henri Blocher writes:

> We must state both that after his revolt mankind remains mankind, and also that mankind has radically changed, that he is but a grisly shadow of himself. Mankind remains the image of God, inviolable and responsible, but has become a contradictory image, one might say a caricature, a witness against himself.[142]

A good illustration of the image of God in fallen man is that of a car windshield that has shattered. The glass remains but it is so damaged that you can no longer see through it. So also with the image of God in fallen mankind. What is particularly lost through sin is our righteousness and holiness. We now are guilty before God, alienated from the God we still know, and we are corrupted in our thoughts and desires. This being the case, the marvelous faculties God has given us now are employed in the service of sin. No longer will we reflect the perfect love of the Trinity in our relationships, but they are damaged and destroyed by a love of self in place of the love for one another. And though we still know God, we raise the fist of rebellion against him. Paul writes that fallen man "does not accept the things of the Spirit of God, for they are folly to him" (1 Corinthians 2:14). Romans 8:7 adds, "the mind that is set on the flesh is hostile to God, for it does not submit to God's law; indeed, it cannot." In short, the image of God has been distorted by total depravity. We remain creatures designed to know God and respond to him in faith and praise. But now fallen man, bearing God's image, responds to divine knowledge by cursing his name and rebelling against his grace.

This dire situation of the image of God shattered by sin raises a final question: can it be restored? And if so, who will do it? Here is yet another vital worldview question: Is there a remedy for the problem of this world?

The answer to this great question is the main subject of the entire Bible, the good news of Jesus Christ, God's Son. There is hope for us in our sin, because of the grace of God which fulfills his original plan for creation. Jesus came to restore our righteousness which was lost through sin against our Maker.

He fulfilled God's law on our behalf and then offered his own life as a sacrifice to God's justice so that we would be forgiven. Romans 3:23–25 explains the great gospel doctrine of justification through faith in Jesus Christ: "for all have sinned and fall short of the glory of God, and are justified by his grace as a gift, through the redemption that is in Christ Jesus, whom God put forward as a propitiation by his blood, to be received by faith."

The good news of salvation in Christ remedies not only our standing with God. God's image involved not only righteousness but holiness of mind, heart, and body. Jesus' saving gift provides the remedy to break sin's power, along with the cleansing of sin's guilt. This is where the language of Genesis 1:27 is echoed in the New Testament teaching that by faith in Jesus we are being "renewed in the spirit of your minds … to put on the new self, created after the likeness of God in true righteousness and holiness" (Ephesians 4:23–24). By the grace of Christ and the power of the Holy Spirit whom he sends, we are born again to a God-honoring life, restored in the image of righteousness and holiness. By the power of the very Spirit who brooded over the waters of the original creation (Genesis 1:2), Paul says, "we all, with unveiled face, beholding the glory of the Lord, are being transformed into [Christ's] image from one degree of glory to another" (2 Corinthians 3:18).

What great joy there is in our justification through faith in Christ! And what hope and purpose there is in the sanctifying work of the Holy Spirit who is conforming us to the image of Christ (Romans 8:29). Henri Blocher exults: "In Jesus Christ, who is both the Son of God and the Image of God, we are restored to our humanity, as true images of our Creator, and more than images; we become God's sons in his Son, by the bond of a new covenant."[143]

Twice God's!

It is tempting to look back on the created image of God which was broken by sin and regret that things will never be the same way with God again. Yet, in the light of God's revealed Word, we see that God's gift in salvation is greater than the original creation blessing, and his purpose in our redemption is a higher communion with him through our union with Christ in faith.

God's attitude is like that of a young boy who bought a kit and spent weeks carefully constructing a treasured sailboat. When it finally was completed, he took it down to the lake. It sailed so beautifully that it kept going, right out of sight. Despite all his efforts, the boy could not find the boat. Several weeks later he was walking past a store window when to his amazement he saw that boat, only it had an expensive price tag on it. He went into the store and explained to the shop-keeper. But the owner said, "I'm sorry, but I paid a great deal of money for this toy boat and I cannot give it to you for free." So the boy took up jobs and worked and worked until he finally had enough money to buy back his boat. Finally, he walked out of the store with his precious boat in his hand. And he said, "Now you are twice mine—once because I made you and once because I bought you."[144]

So it is with God. He created us in his own image, after his own likeness. We belonged to him, but then we were lost in sin. But so great is his love for his people that he sent his

Son, Jesus, to purchase us back by the precious blood of his cross. Now we really are twice his forever—once by creation and again by the cross. However marvelous is the goodness of God in creation, it is only made more wonderful by the grace of God in Jesus Christ. How willing, eager, and excited we should be to bear his image, redeemed and restored in Christ: to know God better, serve him faithfully, and live from now on to the praise of his name.

12   *The Dominion of Man*

Genesis 1:28–31

And God said to them, "Be fruitful and multiply and fill the earth and subdue it and have dominion over the fish of the sea and over the birds of the heavens and over every living thing that moves on the earth" (Genesis 1:28).

THE BOOK OF GENESIS IS NOT THE ONLY STORY OF ORIGINS THAT comes down to us from the ancient world. The great pagan empires also produced tales of the gods and the making of mankind. An example is the Babylonian creation myth, the *Enuma Elish,* which apparently outdates Genesis by several centuries. Some scholars have suggested that Moses drew from the Babylonian stories and have suggested numerous parallels. The reality is that the message of Genesis is entirely opposite of this and other creation myths. To the extent that Moses had the other creation accounts in mind, he wrote Genesis as the one true anti-myth, a counter-cultural message from God himself. Vinoth Ramachandra writes: "A seventh-century Babylonian or a Canaanite in fourteenth-century Ugarit ... would have been shocked by the teaching of Genesis."145 Moses' message in Genesis cried out, "The myths are wrong! Listen to the true God through his Word!"

One way to see this contrast between Genesis and ancient

myths is the relationship between man and God. The *Enuma Elish* sees the creation of man as a pragmatic afterthought, whereas Genesis sets mankind at the pinnacle of God's creation. Marduk, Babylon's chief god, was said to have created man as a slave race to provide for the gods' needs.[146] Genesis declares a transcendent Creator who has no needs but placed his image on all mankind. God then crowned man as his royal servant to exercise dominion over the earth. Instead of creating man to provide food for the gods, Genesis 1:29–30 tells us that God provided food for man to live in his blessing.

Man as God's Vice-Regent

Genesis 1:26 gave mankind the task of rule over the animals: "Let us make man in our image, after our likeness. And let them have dominion over the fish of the sea and over the birds of the heavens and over the livestock and over all the earth." The direct consequence of man's creation in God's image is *our kingly rule on earth.*

Man's dominion is not actually a kingship but a form of vice-regency. Only the Creator is the true king of the world. But God has invested royal authority into the hands of his image-bearers: "God said to them, 'Be fruitful and multiply and fill the earth and subdue it and have dominion over the fish of the sea and over the birds of the heavens and over every living thing that moves on the earth'" (Genesis 1:28). Gordon Wenham writes: "Because man is created in God's image, he is king over nature. He rules the world on God's behalf."[147]

Since man rules on God's behalf we are to keep his standards and goals. Ramachandra writes: "All human beings are called to represent God's kingship through the whole range of human life on earth. And God's rule is not the rule of a despot, but the loving nurture of a caring parent."[148] Man should take God's goodness and bounty as his example: like the Creator we are to do good on the earth.

Genesis 1:28 declares God's blessing on mankind, which includes the Creator's investment in man's ability to fulfill his calling. The pagan myths contain no manward blessing from the gods, but the true God looks on his treasured servants with an aim to bless. In distinction from the lower creatures, God speaks to man, establishing a personal relationship which is in fact the chief blessing God has to give. All that mankind has ever done or will ever do results from his sovereign blessing and should therefore be offered for his praise.

Genesis 1:31 concludes the account of man's creation, and the entire first chapter of Genesis, by declaring that God looked on his work and was pleased. For the seventh time in Genesis 1—seven being a number for divine action—God looks with approval and declares his creation good. Only now the pitch is raised to a higher level: "And God saw everything that he had made, and behold, it was very good. And there was evening and there was morning, the sixth day."

In the first three days, God constructed and provisioned the earth and in the second three days he created living beings to dwell upon it. Now, with the world fashioned and the living creatures created, and with man as God's image-bearer to rule the earth on his behalf, God expresses his full approval. Few statements could so ennoble the human race as God's delight in the dominion of man over the other creatures. In Genesis 1:2, at the very beginning, the earth consisted of a God-designed potential. Now, at Genesis 1:31, God's design has come to fruition in the most remarkable achievement—the creation of heaven and earth. The creation is not only made but is ordered in harmony and peace. Psalm 118 records the antiphonal praise that reflects God's own delight: "Oh give thanks to the LORD, for he is good; for his steadfast love endures forever!" (Psalm 118:1, 29).

Man's Calling to Responsibility

Let's look more closely at man's dominion under God. In particular, we should notice one great principle and two great tasks. The principle enshrined in Genesis 1:28 is *man's responsibility to God for his dominion on earth.*

Accountability to God is implicit in man's vice-regal office. As our authority to rule comes from God, we are also responsible to God. Psalm 24:1 reminds us whose world it is: "The earth is the LORD's and the fullness thereof, the world and those who dwell therein." Man is a steward, not an owner: "we are managers, under the supervision of the chief executive officer; we are not the top of the chain of command."[149]

We are living in a time when many people seek to evade responsibility for their actions. Some people absolve themselves of moral responsibility on the supposed basis of their genes. "I was made this way," they declare, seeking to justify their moral perversities. In other cases, people point to shaping influences so as to deny their responsibility. "I am the product of my environment," people say. "I grew up poor." "I did not have loving parents." "I was exposed to harmful influences." All these things may be true and they undoubtedly involve genuine trials. People are also born with sin tendencies, and Christians should offer compassionate help so far as we are able. But these situations cannot absolve any human being from moral responsibility. Francis Schaeffer argues: "Since God has made man in his own image, man is not caught in the wheels of determinism. Rather man is so great that he can influence history for himself and for others, for this life and the life to come."[150]

It isn't by chance that Adam and Eve's first actions after falling into sin involved covering up their guilt and shifting the blame to others (Genesis 3:7–13). Yet God held them accountable, and Revelation 20:12 assures us that the same will be true in the final judgment: the "books were opened … And the dead were judged by what was written in the books, according to what they had done."

Since God gave mankind dominion, everyone has some dominion for which they are accountable to God. We start out with the vocation, that is calling, of children and are responsible to obey our parents. When a woman marries, she adds the vocation of wife, and a married man takes up the calling of husband. When we have children, we add the vocation of parent. When we take work positions, these constitute vocations with various responsibilities and duties. A pastor is called to the gospel ministry. A doctor is called to healing. A trash collector takes up the important vocation of waste management. At all times, we all exercise some God-given dominion, with authority and duties given to us.

The point is that we are accountable to God for the dominion he has granted us in our vocations. Our dominion always thus has a moral dimension, both in terms of how we exercise authority and to what ends we rule. Since Genesis

1:28–29 focuses on man's dominion over the animals and the earth, we should embrace our obligation to use and employ the earth's resources in a beneficial way, not merely for ourselves but for generations that will follow. When we consider the Creator's pleasure in the goodness of the earth, it is impossible for us to think that he endorses a harmful exploitation of its resources that ruins its future worth! Just as God made a prosperous, harmonious earth, man's stewardship should have similar goals in managing the earth for our descendants who will receive it.

The best way for mankind to be responsible to God is to pay careful attention to his Word. We exercise faithful dominion when we study the Bible, teach God's Word to those under our care, and follow the instructions that pertain to our own particular callings. Micah 6:8 summarizes God's general expectations: "He has told you, O man, what is good; and what does the LORD require of you but to do justice, and to love kindness, and to walk humbly with your God?" Jesus spoke in a similar way, teaching: "let your light shine before others, so that they may see your good works and give glory to your Father who is in heaven" (Matthew 5:16).

Man's Calling to Reproduction

Responsible and accountable dominion is the obvious principle governing the rule of man on earth. Genesis 1:28 also specifies two clear tasks, starting with *man's calling to reproduction*: "And God blessed them. And God said to them, 'Be fruitful and multiply and fill the earth.'" Notice the emphasis that comes by repetition. Being fruitful, multiplying, and filling the earth are basically the same ideas, so we are to take this as God's highlighting on the text.

We can see why multiplication is so important if we recognize how big is the task of exercising dominion on earth. God's work requires more workers! And not just any workers: God needs children raised in Christian homes and churches together with others who respond to the gospel and raise their own children to serve the Lord.

This reproductive mandate is bound to produce a strong Christian emphasis on the institution of marriage. Young Christians should ordinarily be encouraged to marry and have children. Their upbringing should specifically aim at preparing them to be husband-fathers and wife-mothers. These are not the only callings our children will have and they should be prepared for others. But it was God who made fruitfulness in reproduction the first task in man's dominion. Christians and churches should therefore work hard at honoring God in marriage and cultivating a godly, positive sexuality (Hebrews 13:4). This calling to raising children in nurturing, godly home environments is all the more important today as our post-Christian society excels in precisely the opposite, to the destruction of itself.

In recent generations, evangelical Christians have downplayed the priority of child-bearing to marriage, particularly in comparison with the Roman Catholic emphasis on reproduction. We have rightly emphasized that the primary purpose of marriage is God-honoring companionship, so that couples who cannot have children are not in second-class marriages. R. Albert Mohler has pointed out, however, that when Christians de-linked child-bearing from marriage and sex they hastened the acceptance of sexual immorality and homosexual marriage.[151] A balanced view, then, will not make child-bearing the sole definition of marriage but will still emphasize that marriage is designed to fulfill man's first dominion task: "Be fruitful and multiply and fill the earth" (Genesis 1:28).

At a minimum, the Christian community should have a decidedly pro-children mentality. This should be reflected in our value on children, our support of families, our ministries directed to youths, and our prayers. Psalm 127:3–5 speaks powerfully of the biblical attitude:

> Behold, children are a heritage from the LORD, the fruit of the womb a reward. Like arrows in the hand of a warrior are the children of one's youth. Blessed is the man who fills his quiver with them! He shall not be put to shame when he speaks with his enemies in the gate.

These verses do not mean that Christian couples who cannot have children are under a divine curse or are otherwise second-class. Indeed, such believers often make themselves invaluable co-parents to all the children in the church. Moreover, Psalm 127 does not mean that Christians should compete over the vastness of their families. It is a legitimate concern to ask how many children a family can afford to raise and some believers have callings from God that make large families inadvisable. Yet Mohler rightly responds to the creation mandate with this affirmation: "evangelicals must affirm that every *marriage* must be open to the gift of children and that, should pregnancy occur, it is to be seen as an unconditional gift rather than as an imposition."[152]

In addition to valuing children, the Christian worldview promotes an outlook that is keenly motivated to honoring and promoting life in general. Historically, Christians have been at the forefront in opposing such brutal practices as slavery and torture. Remembering our dominion mandate over the living creatures, Christians have also opposed animal cruelty. Vinoth Ramachandra writes: "The much-maligned Puritans of sixteenth century England campaigned tirelessly against cruel practices such as bear-baiting and cockfighting." He quotes Horace Walpole as remarking in 1760 that an acquaintance was "turning Methodist; for, in the middle of conversation, he arose, and opened a window to let out a moth."[153]

It is noteworthy that in Genesis 1:29–30, God provided plants for man's food. God's original design in creation called for even the animals to respect the life of other living creatures: "And to every beast of the earth and to every bird of the heavens and to everything that creeps on the earth, everything that has the breath of life, I have given every green plant for food." This arrangement would change after the entry of sin, as God gave man the animals for food (Genesis 9:3). But the reverence for "everything that has the breath of life" (Genesis 1:30), ought to shape a Christian pro-life attitude that is reflected in our approach to life in general.

Man's Calling to Work

If man's first task is to reproduce, second is *his calling to work*. We see this calling in man's responsibility to the earth: "subdue it and have dominion over it." In Genesis 3, after the fall, God gives the curse of frustration and futility in our work. But work itself results from creation, not the fall.

The attitude of many people today is to regard work as an unpleasant necessity. Therefore, they hoard their wealth so as to retire at the earliest possible age in order to indulge themselves with pleasure. But work is good and is vital to our earthly dominion.

The word for "subdue" (Hebrew, *kabas*) involves the exertion of strength. Anyone who has engaged in farming can tell you it involves hard manual labor with the land. Even apart from the effects of sin, diligent work in any field calls for the forceful exertion of our faculties and time in order to accomplish worthwhile things. Christians should not merely dabble at our work but, as Ecclesiastes 9:10 tells us, "Whatever your hand finds to do, do it with your might." Christian youths should work hard in school to develop useful knowledge and skills, and all believers should approach our careers with a godly ambition and determination.

It is noteworthy that while the animals are given food to eat, Genesis 1:29 says that God gave man not only food but also seed: "Behold, I have given you every plant yielding seed that is on the face of all the earth, and every tree with seed in its fruit." This giving of seed indicates that man is distinctively called to the work of agriculture. Alasdair Paine comments: "Animals forage; we normally farm. This is a simple and rather basic example of the way we exercise our kingly rule. The animals graze and hunt; we plough the fields and scatter [seeds]."[154] More broadly, this means that man is called to the management of resources and the building of useful enterprises. God's calling leads us into collaborate efforts that result in societies of various kinds. This means that it is a God-honoring life to raise children and build a business, participate in growing a church, or play a role in civic affairs. In Genesis 2, we encounter Adam as the first scientist, called to study and name the animals. Humans exercise dominion by applying our intelligence in addition to our brawn. We cultivate the arts of communication and play a role in complex endeavors designed to order the nature that God has placed under our care for things of value, usefulness, and beauty.

At the same, believers must avoid the trap of worshiping our work and glorifying our achievements, which becomes idolatry. Rather, we are to offer our work to God for his service and praise. At the entrance to the Cavendish Laboratory in Cambridge, England, a renowned center for experimental physics, the words of Psalm 111:2 are written: "The works of the LORD are great, sought out of all them that have pleasure therein."[155] Just as the biblical worldview resulted in the so-called "Protestant work ethic" that was so important to the achievements of the Christian West, a God-glorifying perspective will grant nobility and purpose to any vocational calling, whether it is glamorous or overlooked in the eyes of the world. The Christian rule for work is stated aptly in Colossians 3:17: "whatever you do, in word or deed, do everything in the name of the Lord Jesus, giving thanks to God the Father through him."

Serving the Dominion of Christ

How blessed is man through the dominion granted to him by God, and how important is every human being in the role they are given by God to play in the work of the world. This also means that the character of men and women, to whom such authority is granted, is vitally important to God. Imagine what would happen if these vice-regents of God should fall into sin? We do not need to imagine this, of course. For man has fallen and, ever since, the deadly poison of evil has infected the dominion of man, so often making the world a place where blessing is hard to find.

Today, there are whole cultures where the very eco-system has been destroyed by man. The island of Haiti, for instance, despite the lush condition of nearby islands, is a virtual desert where crops are barely able to grow. To ask how this could happen, one need only consider the Satanic culture of voodoo that dominates its history. On a moral and psychological level, the same can be said of some of the most affluent communities in prosperous America, where egoism and sensualism have ravaged so many families that depression, domestic violence, and despair are widespread, especially among youths. Under sin, rule becomes exploitation. Man in sin has become a tyrant and invader, often blaming God for the destruction that is rightly laid at his own feet.

In what Paul labeled "the present evil age" (Galatians 1:4), God has given a new cultural mandate to the new creation that is the Christian church. We find it in Jesus' Great Commission: "Go therefore and make disciples of all nations, baptizing them in the name of the Father and of the Son and of the Holy Spirit, teaching them to observe all that I have commanded you" (Matthew 28:19–20). In addition to the creation mandates of reproduction and work, Christians now have the redemptive mandate of gospel missions. Jesus said to the Father about his followers: "As you sent me into the world, so I have sent them into the world" (John 17:18).

An excellent example for our missions is the approach set

by Moses in writing Genesis. I have noted that Genesis was written as an anti-myth against the backdrop of the false creation myths of the ancient pagan world. Moses was saying in Genesis: "Do not believe the false message of the world and its myths! Believe in the God who has spoken in his Word!" Christians today are to do the same. We speak into a world dominated by so many deadly falsehoods. There is the myth of evolution and its ruthless idea of human progress. There is the myth of sensual indulgence, which promises pleasure but enslaves and destroys. There are the myths of the entertainment industry, which tell us that violating God's commands will be wholesome and good, and urges young people to live according to their selfish desires. Against all of these and more, Christians cry out, "Do not believe the false myths! Turn anew to the Creator and his Word, to the blessing of him who gave us life and work, and the redemption from sin that came through the gift of his Son, Jesus, and the blood of his cross."

Isaac Watts put in song, based on Psalm 72, the promise of Christ's kingdom on which his people rely and to which we now work:

> Jesus shall reign where'er the sun
>   does his successive journeys run;
> His kingdom stretch from shore to shore,
>   till moons shall wax and wane no more.

As the earth was blessed by man's dominion prior to sin, how blessed are sinners who come under the heavenly dominion of Jesus Christ:

> Blessings abound where'er he reigns;

> the pris'ner leaps to lose his chains;
> The weary find eternal rest,
>   and all the sons of want are blest.[156]

What good work it is to spread the gospel message of Jesus! And how joyful it is to be fruitful and multiply as believers, serving God as he fills the earth not only with redeemed children of God, but with the promise of ultimate success to the dominion begun in Genesis 1. Isaiah 11:9 foretells the destiny to which we so confidently labor by the mighty grace of a saving God:

> They shall not hurt or destroy in all my holy mountain; for the earth shall be full of the knowledge of the LORD as the waters cover the sea.

13   *The Sabbath Rest*

Genesis 2:1–3

So God blessed the seventh day and made it holy, because on it God rested from all his work that he had done in creation (Genesis 2:3).

THEY SAY THAT IMITATION IS THE HIGHEST FORM OF FLATTERY. Man the creature is called in Genesis to imitate God the Creator, giving him honor and glory in this way. God ruled the creation and man is to do the same thing. God commanded: "subdue [the earth] and have dominion" (Genesis 1:28). Likewise, as God filled the earth with living creatures, so also man was charged: "Be fruitful and multiply and fill the earth" (Genesis 1:28). This principle of bearing God's image by imitation carries over to the creation account's final scene: "And on the seventh day God finished his work that he had done, and he rested on the seventh day from all his work that he had done" (Genesis 2:2). Genesis 2:3 adds that "God blessed the seventh day and made it holy," establishing a creation mandate for our Sabbath observance. Mankind is to imitate God not only in work but also in rest!

God's Seventh Day Rest

It is unfortunate that the Bible's first chapter division isolates

169

the conclusion of Genesis 1's creation account by placing the seventh day in Genesis 2. This division is not seen in the original texts, the chapter and verse divisions only appearing as a late medieval innovation. The chapter division notwithstanding, Genesis 2:2's statement marks the conclusion to the creation account: "on the seventh day God finished his work that he had done."

We have had an exciting tour of the week of creation, when God made the heavens and the earth. Finally, this most dramatic of weeks ends on the seventh day: "Thus the heavens and the earth were finished, and all the host of them" (Genesis 2:1). God looked on all the varied creatures gathered together rendering praise to his marvelous glory: from stars above to fish in the sea, and with man to bear his image. The creation was not a static collection but a marvelous machine now set in motion, with its natural laws and seasons, all designed to make life on earth possible, as a stage to manifest the glory of God in history.

While each of the prior six days records creative activity by God, the seventh day was one of rest: "And on the seventh day God finished his work that he had done, and he rested on the seventh day from all his work that he had done" (Genesis 2:2). Let's be clear that God did not rest because he was worn out from the heavy lifting of creating stars and planets! Rather, his work in creation was finished. The word for "rested" (Hebrew, *shabat*) has the primary meaning of *ceasing*. Having finished his creation, God stopped from the work he had been doing. God would continue working after this first Sabbath rest, and the rest of the Bible records his ongoing providence in governing the history that would come. But, for now, the great work of creation was completed, the heavens and the earth were made and populated, and God ceased from this work.

Genesis 2:3 responds to God's rest by declaring, "God blessed the seventh day." Previously, God's blessing rested on living creatures, like the fish, birds, and mankind (Genesis 1:22, 28). Now, as God blesses the seventh day it is evident that this too is for the benefit of his creatures. The days of God's creation work were declared good. But his seventh day of rest is declared blessed, marking it out as special. Clearly, we are to think differently about the seventh day compared to the other six. God's Sabbath thus challenges the way that people think today. We think of work as the activity that accomplishes the most things, whereas God sees his rest as especially profitable. David Wilkinson comments that "in the natural world fruitfulness is ... associated with rest. A field cannot be farmed constantly, but needs a period of lying fallow to ensure continuing fruitfulness. Written into God's creation is the necessity of rest."[157] As God sees it, entering his rest is key to a fruitful and blessed life.

Genesis 2:3 establishes the seventh day rest as a creation ordinance to be perpetually observed: "God blessed the seventh day and made it holy, because on it God rested from all his work that he had done in creation." For God to declare something "holy" is to set it apart for himself. Later in Scripture, God will call numerous things holy, including the temple, its priests, and Israel's feast days. The very first thing that God sanctified was the seventh day, noting the significance of the seventh-day rest.

The reality of the Sabbath rest as a perpetual ordinance for all creation is amplified by the Fourth Commandment, after Israel had been delivered from bondage in Egypt. It reads:

> Remember the Sabbath day, to keep it holy. Six days you shall labor, and do all your work, but the seventh day is a Sabbath to the LORD your God. On it you shall not do any work, you, or your son, or your daughter, your male servant, or your female servants, or your livestock, or the sojourner who is within your gates (Exodus 20:8–10).

Note how the Fourth Commandment takes up a universal scope, marking its application not just to old covenant Israel but to all persons. Its rationale links back to Genesis 2:3, when "the LORD blessed the Sabbath day and made it holy" (Exodus 20:11). Like the First Commandment against idolatry and the Sixth Commandment against murder—indeed, like all ten—the Sabbath is a perpetual mandate rooted in God's character. John Calvin summarizes that Genesis 2:3 "is nothing else than a solemn consecration, by which God claims for himself the meditations and employments of men on the seventh day."[158]

God's Sovereign Rest

When you and I rest, we usually are letting other people take charge. Not so with God! The Bible develops from God's rest a rich theology of divine sovereignty. God's Sabbath rest, we find, is a *sovereign* rest.

God entered his rest on the seventh day by taking up his throne and entering his reign over all creation. We can see this connection in the Bible accounts involving the construction and completion of Israel's temple. Solomon took seven years to build this wonder of the ancient world, dedicated it on the seventh month, and gave a dedicatory prayer consisting of seven petitions. G. K. Beale comments that "the temple appears to have been modelled on the seven-day creation of the world."[159] Moreover, the temple was adorned with creation images drawn from the Garden of Eden. David described the temple as "a house of rest for the ark of the covenant of the LORD and for the footstool of our God" (1 Chronicles 28:2). Later, when Solomon actually brought the ark into the holy of holies, he cried: "now arise, O LORD God, and go to your resting place" (2 Chronicles 6:41). The temple thus declared God's rest in terms of his reign on earth. Reflecting on these links between the temple and Genesis 2:2, John Walton notes: "God did not set up the cosmos so that only people will have a place. He also sets up the cosmos to serve as his temple in which he will find rest in the order and equilibrium he has established."[160]

Walton provides an apt illustration for how we should think about God entering his rest after finishing the work of creation. In order to be elected President of the United States, a candidate must do the work of campaigning in order to receive votes. After he has been elected, the campaign is over and the new President takes up residence in the White House. He "settles in" and begins to accomplish the goals for which he sought office. It is in this way that God entered his rest over creation on the seventh day, not to relax but to launch his plans for history.[161]

The point is that God's rest declares his sovereign reign over all the history that will follow his creation of the heavens and the earth. It is in this respect that we should understand the significance of the fact that this seventh day is not marked off, like the six others, by "evening and morning." The point is not that the original seventh day had no end—the Fourth Commandment clearly sees it as a normal day—but that it *symbolized* a sovereign reign that will last forever. God's temple in Jerusalem declared his sovereign presence and rule to save his covenant people. Likewise, God's creation rest declared his eternal sovereignty over all people, places, and events in the history of the world.

It is most appropriate that God, as the Maker of heaven and earth, should exercise his full rights of ownership. Moreover, the attributes that enabled God to create the universe out of nothing were not suspended when he entered his rest. Rather, history reveals the full expression of God's omnipotence, omniscience, and omnipresence.

This absolute sovereignty offers great comfort to those who have entered into a saving relationship with God through faith in his Son. Having stated God's sovereignty over us, Jesus said, "Fear not, therefore" (Matthew 10:31). It was likewise because of the sovereignty of God in his eternal rest that Paul could exclaim:

I am sure that neither death nor life, nor angels nor rulers, nor things present nor things to come, nor powers, nor height nor depth, nor anything else in all creation, will be able to separate us from the love of God in Christ Jesus our Lord (Romans 8:38–39).

God's Saving Rest

The New Testament adds to God's sovereignty the idea of God's *saving* rest. We find this in Hebrews chapter 4, where, citing Psalm 95, the author looks back to Israel's entry into the Promised Land as entering God's rest. Hebrews reflects from this that God's rest on the seventh day was symbolic of a future rest of which the land of Canaan was itself a type. The true Sabbath rest is the salvation that God offers through Jesus Christ. The final rest without evening or morning is the glorious eternal age that Jesus will bring when he returns from heaven to earth. In this sense, God blessed the seventh day and made it holy to bear testimony to the eternal rest we enter through Christ's work of redemption.

God entered his rest not by subduing monsters and lesser gods, as in the Babylonian creation myth, but by ordering and filling the creation he had made. Jesus did, however, achieve rest for us through the overthrow of hostile powers. He conquered sin and Satan through his atoning death on the cross and overthrew death by his glorious resurrection from the grave. It is through faith in Jesus, therefore, that we enter into his rest.

Hebrews was written to people who professed faith in Jesus. Yet he urged them to make sure that they entered into Christ's rest by believing his gospel (Hebrews 4:1–3). For us, the final rest is more than the present salvation we enjoy, including the forgiveness of our sins. The salvation rest is the eternal life that Jesus offers beyond both the grave and at the end of history for those who persevere in faith. Hebrews 4:9 thus declares, "there remains a Sabbath rest for the people of God." We enter the salvation rest by believing in Christ and await the full and eternal rest when he returns. The final reality of which our weekly Sabbaths are a foretaste is still to come: the eternal age of glory for which Christ is working now through the spread of his gospel.

Keeping the Sabbath Rest

Since the seventh-day rest was made holy by God at the climax of creation and then highlighted as one of the Ten Commandments, its ongoing validity is clear. Christians do not, however, rest on the Sabbath in the manner of Old Testament Israelites under the threat of the penalty of death (Exodus 31:14). Instead, Christians receive the Sabbath rest as a blessing from God and offer our day back to him as holy to the Lord. In pursuit of biblical Sabbath observance, I would suggest three categories in which Christians should keep the Sabbath holy: through corporate worship, as a testimony to the final rest that is yet to come, and as a holy source of refreshment and enjoyment in the Lord.

First, since God entered his rest by taking up his throne of sovereignty, the most important activity for Christians is to join together as a church to exalt him in gathered *worship*. Psalm 47:6–7 sets our response to his enthronement: "Sing praises to God, sing praises! Sing praises to our King, sing praises! For God is the King of all the earth; sing praises with a psalm!"

One of the ways to think of the difference between Christian worship and Old Testament worship is to note the change to the day on which we worship the Lord. In both Acts 20:7 and 1 Corinthians 16:2, the New Testament notes that the early church gathered for worship on the first day of the week (Sunday, versus Saturday). This change reflects the transformative achievement of Christ's resurrection. G. K.

Beale explains: "Christ's resurrection was the beginning of the new creation and the consummation of Christ's 'rest' as king."[162] Israel's seven-day feasts concluded with a special or great Sabbath on the eighth day, which occurred on the first day of the week and which the New Testament sees as symbolic of Christ's saving reign. On one of these eighth- (or first-) day occasions, Jesus called out: "If anyone thirsts, let him come to me and drink. Whoever believes in me, as the Scripture has said, 'Out of his heart will flow rivers of living water'" (John 7:37–38). Christians respond to this offer in faith by setting apart the first day of the week to gather in worship. We not only commemorate his resurrection but we meet with Christ and gain spiritual nourishment through God's Word, prayer, and the sacraments.

The vital importance of weekly attendance in the gathered worship of the church cannot be overstated. The fourth commandment looks back to Genesis 2:3 in saying that "the Lord blessed the Sabbath day and made it holy" (Exodus 20:11). Christians should therefore conceive of Sunday worship as a spiritual feast, as well as a solemn obligation. How greatly Christians cheapen the Sabbath day when we come to church wondering only what we "can get out of it." If we will worship with a primary aim of giving God the glory he deserves as our sovereign Lord and saving Father, we ourselves will be the first to be blessed.

The great missionary John G. Paton was used by God to convert an entire island of formerly savage cannibals in the South Pacific. Paton looked on their reverent and biblical worship as the crowning achievement of Christ's mighty grace and correctly identified Sabbath-keeping as a sign of their spiritual maturity. Once, when separated from them, Paton lamented, "my soul longed after the holy Sabbaths of Aniwa!"[163] We should likewise lament being absent from God's house on the day of his appointment, when his church gathers together in reverent praise and to receive grace from Christ's own hand.

A second purpose in Sabbath-keeping is as *a testimony* to the final rest in the age to come with Christ. The Sabbath day is a sign of God's salvation. It is on this ground that some Christians believe that Sabbath-keeping expired with the old covenant, together with the temple and sacrifices. Since the reality has come in Christ, they reason, the sign is no longer valid. The problem with this view is that the Sabbath is not a sign only of Christ's first coming but also of his second coming and its eternal rest in blessing. This is why Hebrews 4:9 states, "there remains a Sabbath rest for the people of God."

In setting aside one day out of seven for God, we bear testimony first to ourselves. How easy it is for Christians to become so enmeshed in this world that we forget that we are meant for a better world to come! As a royal priesthood and holy nation (1 Peter 2:9), Christians are set apart by God from the world and its ways. By turning aside from worldly affairs one day out of seven, we remind ourselves of our higher calling and privileges. Ezekiel 20:12 says: "I gave them my Sabbaths, as a sign between me and them, that they might know that I am the LORD who sanctifies them." Sabbath-observing Christians are also a sign to the unbelieving world in its mad pursuit of work and pleasure. As we pull back from worldly activities, we reveal that there is a special people in this world, the Christian church, who are devoted to God and are freed from bondage to work and recreation.

Third, Christians keep the Lord's Sabbath as *refreshment* from their worldly labor, by devoting themselves to spiritual engagement with the Lord. Here we return to the creation principle of man imitating his Creator. God "rested on the seventh day from all his work that he had done" (Genesis 2:2). Now we are to receive the Lord's Day as a spiritual blessing and offer it holy to God. John Calvin explained that "God did not command men simply to keep holiday" on the Sabbath, "but rather that they, being released from all other business, might the more readily apply their minds to the Creator of the world."[164]

Isaiah 58 provides a guide to Sabbath-observance in the final section of that book which looks ahead to the new covenant era. Speaking of our Christian times, he urges believers to "call the Sabbath a delight and the holy day of the LORD honorable" (Isaiah 58:13). We honor the Lord's Day by "not going your own ways, or seeking your own pleasure, or talking idly." This is in keeping with the Fourth Commandment's instruction to refrain from our work. A good rule is to set aside whatever is your weekday vocation, whether construction, study, or meeting with clients. As Jesus showed in confronting the legalism of the Pharisees, there are works of necessity and mercy—such as providing medical care, essential government services, and preaching—that must still be performed on Sundays. But as far as possible, we should set aside our work and worldly recreations to offer a whole day to God and to spiritual enrichment. Isaiah 58:14 concludes with a promised blessing. If you "take delight in the LORD," God says, "I will make you ride on the heights of the earth."

But is it really possible to set aside a whole day from work? Can students really set aside their books on the Lord's Day? Don't businessmen have to work every day to meet their quotas? What is the answer to these and similar questions? It is to remember that by observing the Sabbath we confess our faith in a God who is sovereign. If we did not have a sovereign and gracious God, it would probably be true that we have to work all the time without ceasing, like Israel in the mud-pits of Egypt. The same is true for believers who devote themselves to worldly recreations on Sundays at the expense of spiritually enriching activities. But the reality is that on the seventh day God entered his rest, taking up his sovereignty for the sake of his people. We can set our work aside, resting in him and devoting ourselves to Christian worship, godly fellowship, spiritual conversation, and holy meditation. Indeed, the more we joyfully look upon the Sabbath not only as a holy duty but as a blessing provided by God, the more in line we will be with his creation design.

It Is Finished!

The fact that "on the seventh day God finished his work that he had done" and then rested (Genesis 2:2), is the best of good news to us. It shows that our God finishes what he begins. God was able to complete the creation work because of his infinite power, sublime wisdom, and faithfulness. When we trust our souls to his care, believing on Jesus, we can be sure that God will finish our salvation, bringing us with him into the eternal glory. It is because God is a finisher that we have assurance of salvation through faith in Jesus. Paul exclaimed: "I am sure of this, that he who began a good work in you will bring it to completion at the day of Jesus Christ" (Philippians 1:6).

God is so determined to finish what he began that even the sinful messes of his people won't stop him. Adam fell into sin, earning God's wrath, but God promised him a Savior who would redeem sinners by dying in their place (see Genesis 3:15, 21). Jesus came to do what God had promised. He took up a human nature so that he could save fallen men and women. He fulfilled all the prophecies so we would recognize him as God's Savior. Then by dying on the cross, Jesus did everything necessary to fulfill God's saving will. As he prepared to die, solving the problem of our sin, Jesus exclaimed, "It is finished" (John 19:30). We can therefore know that God has accomplished everything needed to restore us to his love.

The first verse of Genesis 1 showed us that history had a beginning, with God as the Creator. The final verses of the creation account prove that this God is the finisher of all that he began. This means that his promises are all going to come true. The future he envisions in the Bible is certain to arrive. The Savior who died on the cross will return to reign at the final judgment.

Believing in Jesus is at the heart of the Christian worldview we discover and begin in Genesis 1. Genesis 1 tells us that we live in a world created by God and that we are his special image-bearing creatures. Before too long, Genesis 3 will tell us what kind of world we now live in, a world made good but scarred by the ravages of sin. The Christian worldview sees the answer to this greatest of all problems in the coming of Jesus to be our Savior. And to what does Jesus call us by faith? Nothing less than the saving and eternal rest of the sovereign God who loves us. He invites us now, saying: "Come to me, all who labor and are heavy laden, and I will give you rest" (Matthew 11:28).

Endnotes

Chapter 1.

1 Cited from Alasdair Paine, *The First Chapters of Everything* (Ross-Shire, UK: Christian Focus, 2014), 17.

2 Derek Thomas, "The Bible's First Word," in Richard D. Phillips, ed. *God, Adam, & You: Biblical Creation Defended and Applied* (Phillipsburg, NJ: P&R, 2015), 3.

3 Ravi Zacharias, *Can Man Live Without God* (Nashville: Thomas Nelson, 1994), 92.

4 G. Ch. Aalders, *Genesis*, 2 vols. (Grand Rapids, MI: Zondervan, 1981), 1:52.

5 G. Campbell Morgan, *The Westminster Pulpit*, 10 vols. (Grand Rapids, MI: Baker, 1906, reprint 1995), 5:322.

6 Alec Motyer, *Look to the Rock* (Leicester: IVP, 1996), 67.

7 Stephen Hawking, *A Brief History of Time* (New York: Bantam, 1998), 38.

8 R. Kent Hughes, *Genesis*, Preaching the Word (Wheaton, IL: Crossway, 2004), 20.

9 Henri Blocher, *In the Beginning: The Opening Chapters of Genesis* (Leicester, UK: InterVarsity, 1984), 61.

Chapter 2.

10   W. M. Hetherington, *History of the Westminster Assembly of Divines* (Edinburgh: James Gemmell, 1878), 369.

11   Ibid. 369–70.

12   Charles H. Spurgeon, *New Park Street Pulpit*, 6 vols. (Pasadena, TX: Pilgrim Publications, 1975), 1:1–2.

13   J. I. Packer, *Knowing God* (Downers Grove, IL: InterVarsity Press, 1973), 14–15.

14   Peter Lewis, *The Message of the Living God*, The Bible Speaks Today (Downers Grove, IL: InterVarsity, 2000), 28.

15   Quoted in Wentzel Van Huyssteen, ed., *Encyclopedia of Science and Religion* (New York: Macmillan, 2003), 621.

16   Francis A. Schaeffer, *Genesis in Space and Time*, in *Collected Works of Francis A. Schaeffer* (Wheaton, IL: Crossway, 1985), 2:11.

17   A. W. Pink, *The Attributes of God* (Grand Rapids, MI: Baker, 1975), 46.

18   Stephen Charnock, *The Existence and Attributes of God*, 2 vols. (Grand Rapids, MI: Baker, 1853, reprint 1996), 2:15.

19   A. W. Tozer, *The Knowledge of the Holy* (San Francisco, CA: HarperCollins, 1961, reprint 1992), 101.

20   William Still, *Theological Studies in Genesis and Romans* (Ross-shire, UK: Christian Focus, 2000), 12.

21   Bruce Milne, *The Message of Heaven and Hell*, The Bible Speaks Today (Downers Grove, IL: InterVarsity, 2002), 38.

22   Stuart K. Hine, "How Great Thou Art", 1949.

23 Pink, *Attributes of God*, 51.

24 Hine, "How Great Thou Art".

Chapter 3.

25 John Calvin, *Calvin's Commentaries*, 22 vols. (Grand Rapids, MI: Baker, 2009), 2:73.

26 The preceding paragraphs were loosely adapted from R. C. Sproul, "The Self-Existence of God," *Philadelphia Conference on Reformed Theology*, audio recording, 1988

27 Herman Bavinck, *Reformed Dogmatics*, 4 vols. (Grand Rapids, MI: Baker, 2009), 2:151.

28 James Henley Thornwell, *The Collected Writings of James Henley Thornwell*, 3 vols. (Vestavia Hills, AL: Solid Ground Christian Books, 1901, reprint 2004), 3:203.

29 R. C. Sproul, "The Self-Existence of God," *Philadelphia Conference on Reformed Theology*, audio recording, 1988.

30 Thornwell, *Collected Writings*, 2:198.

31 *The Westminster Confession of Faith*, 2.2.

32 Tozer, *The Knowledge of the Holy*, 54.

33 Thornwell, *Collected Writings*, 2:198.

34 A. W. Pink, *The Attributes of God* (Grand Rapids, MI: Baker, 1975), 37.

35 Philip Graham Ryken: *Discovering God in Stories from the Bible* (Wheaton, IL: Crossway, 1999), 70.

36 Thornwell, *Collected Writings*, 2:202.

37 Wilhelmus à Brakel, *The Christian's Reasonable Service*, 4 vols. (Grand Rapids, MI: Reformation Heritage, 1992), 1:101.

Chapter 4.

38   Edward S. Creasy, *Fifteen Decisive Battles of the World: From Marathon to Waterloo* (New York, NY: Dorset Press, 1987), 36–56.

39   John Calvin, *Genesis* (Edinburgh: Banner of Truth Trust, 1554, reprint 1992), 71.

40   C. John Collins, *Genesis 1–4: A Linguistic, Literary, and Theological Commentary* (Phillipsburg, NJ: P&R, 2006), 54.

41   It was widely supposed that this fall of Satan is described in Isaiah 14:12–15, which begins, "How are you fallen from heaven, O Day Star, son of Dawn!" It is not at all certain, however, that this refers to Satan, since the original context is directed to the Babylonian conqueror Nebuchadnezzar.

42   H. C. Leupold, *Exposition of Genesis, Volume 1: Chapters 1–19* (Grand Rapids, MI: Baker, 1942), 46.

43   John Sailhamer, *Genesis*, in *The Expositor's Bible Commentary*, 12 volumes (Grand Rapids, Zondervan, 1990), 2:24.

44   Quoting Russell Humphreys. Andrew S. Kulikovsky, *Creation, Fall, Restoration: A Biblical Theology of Creation* (Ross-Shire, UK, 2009), 124.

45   Ibid.

46   R. Kent Hughes, *Genesis*, Preaching the Word (Wheaton, IL: Crossway, 2004), 22.

Chapter 5.

47   Leon Morris, *The Gospel According to John* (Revised), The New International Commentary on the New Testament (Grand Rapids, MI: Eerdmans, 1995), 66.

48 *Westminster Confession of Faith*, II.3.

49 Sidney Greidanus, *Preaching Christ from Genesis* (Grand Rapids, MI: Eerdmans, 2007), 56.

50 Mark E. Hunt, 1978, adapted verses for John Wesley, "Come, Thou Long-Expected Jesus", 1744.

51 Gerhard von Rad, *Genesis*, The Old Testament Library (Philadelphia, PA: Westminster, 1961), 50.

52 Walter Brueggemann, *Genesis, Interpretation* (Atlant, GA: John Knox, 1982), 30.

53 Alasdair Paine, *The First Chapters of Everything* (Ross-Shire, UK: Christian Focus, 2014), 32.

54 Andrew S. Kulikovsky, *Creation, Fall, Restoration: A Biblical Theology of Creation* (Ross-Shire, UK, 2009), 124.

55 Gordon J. Wenham, *Genesis 1–15*, Word Biblical Commentary (Dallas, TX: Word Books, 1987), 18.

56 John Calvin, *Sermons on Genesis Chapters 1–11*, trans. Rob Boy McGregor (Edinburgh: Banner of Truth, 2009), 25.

Chapter 6.

57 Quoted in Edward J. Young, *Studies in Genesis One* (Phillipsburg, NJ: P&R, 1964), 43.

58 Ibid.

59 Ibid.

60 Vern S. Poythress, *Christian Interpretations of Genesis 1* (Phillipsburg, NJ: P&R, 2013), 13.

61 Young, *Studies in Genesis One*, 53–54.

62   Mark E. Ross, "The Framework Hypothesis: An Interpretation of Genesis 1:1–2:3," in Joseph A. Pipa, Jr., and David W. Hall, eds. *Did God Create in 6 Days?* (White Hall, WV: Tolle Lege Press, 1999), 115.

63   Poythress, *Christian Interpretations of Genesis 1*, 14.

64   John Calvin, *Institutes of the Christian Religion*, Henry Beveridge, trans. (Peabody, MA: Hendrickson, 2008), I.6.1.

65   Young, *Studies in Genesis*, 54.

66   Andrew S. Kulikovsky, *Creation, Fall, Restoration: A Biblical Theology of Creation* (Ross-Shire, UK: Christian Focus, 2009), 162.

67   For a more thorough analysis of the day-age concordance theory, see Kulikovsky, *Creation, Fall, Restoration*, 148–153, and Pipa & Hall, *Did God Create in 6 Days?* 177–178.

68   Young, *Studies in Genesis One*, 78, n. 73.

69   Henri Blocher, *In the Beginning: The Opening Chapters of Genesis* (Leicester, UK: InterVarsity Press, 1984), 50.

70   Meredith G. Kline, "Because It Had Not Rained," *Westminster Theological Journal* 20 (1958), 155–56.

71   Ross, "The Framework Hypothesis," in Pipa and Hall, *Did God Create in 6 Days?* 127.

72   Meredith G. Kline, "Genesis", in *The New Bible Commentary*, third edition, Donald Guthrie, ed. (Downers Grove, IL: InterVarsity, 1970), 82–83.

73   For a full and detailed refutation of the Framework Hypothesis, see Young, *Studies in Genesis One*, 43–105, and Pipa, *Did God Create in 6 Days?* 151–196.

74   Grammatically, Genesis 1 employs the *waw consecutive* construction with the prefix *waw* attached to verbs. This signifies consecutive historical narrative, i.e. literal historical events.

75   Noel Weeks, *The Sufficiency of Scripture* (Edinburgh: Banner of Truth, 1988), 107.

76   Blocher, *In the Beginning*, 48.

77   Geerhardus Vos, *Reformed Dogmatics*, trans. Richard B. Gaffin, Jr., 4 vols. (Grand Rapids, MI: Eerdmans, 2014), 1:161

78   Derek Kidner, *Genesis*, Tyndale Old Testament Commentaries (Nottingham: InterVarsity Press, 1967), 61.

79   See previous discussion of this grammatical structure on page 50.

80   Pipa, *Did God Create in 6 Days?* 180–81. This section follows Pipa's argument in pages 179–187,

81   C. Stuart Patterson, "Evidences for a Young Earth," in Pipa and Hall, *Did God Create in 6 Days?* 316–17.

82   Poythress, *Christian Interpretations of Genesis 1*, 7.

Chapter 7.

83   Richard Dawkins, *The God Delusion* (New York, NY: Houghton, Mifflin, Harcourt, 2006), 113.

84   Carl Sagan, *Cosmos* (New York, NY: Random House, 1980), 4.

85   David Livingston notes: "The emphasis in the Hebrew word *raqia* is not on the material itself but on the act of spreading out." Cited by Andrew S. Kulikovsky, *Creation, Fall,*

Restoration: A Biblical Theology of Creation (Ross-Shire, UK, Christian Focus, 2009), 131.

86   William Still, *Theological Studies in Genesis and Romans* (Ross-shire, UK: Christian Focus, 2000), 16.

87   Meredith G. Kline, *Kingdom Prologue: Genesis Foundations for a Covenantal Worldview* (Eugene, OR: Wipf & Stock, 2006), 29.

88   Peter S. Jones, *One or Two: Seeing a World of Difference* (Escondido, CA: Main Entry Editions, 2010).

89   Henri Blocher, *In the Beginning: The Opening Chapters of Genesis* (Leicester, UK: InterVarsity Press, 1984), 72.

90   Peter Jones, *The Pagan Heart of Today's Culture* (Phillipsburg, NJ: P&R, 2014), 9.

91   John Lennon, "Imagine" (Downtown Music Publishing, 1971).

92   John Currid, *Genesis: Volume 1, Genesis 1:1–25:18* (Darlington: UK: Evangelical Press, 2003), 70.

93   Blocher, *In the Beginning*, 67.

94   Umberto Cassuto, *A Commentary on the Book of Genesis: Part 1, From Adam to Noah, Genesis 1–6:8* (Skokie, IL: Varda Books, 1944, reprint 2005), 40.

95   R. Kent Hughes, *Genesis, Preaching the Word* (Wheaton, IL: Crossway, 2004), 29.

Chapter 8.

96   John Currid, *Genesis: Volume 1, Genesis 1:1–25:18* (Darlington: UK: Evangelical Press, 2003), 71.

97   Victor Hamilton, *The Books of Genesis, Chapters 1–17*, New International Commentary on the Old Testament (Grand Rapids, MI: Eerdmans, 1990), 126.

98 Phillip E. Johnson, "The Church of Darwin," *The Wall Street Journal*, Aug. 16, 1999. http://www.wsj.com/articles/SB934759227734378961. Accessed 8 February 2018. Subscription required to read full article.

99 Julian Huxley, *Essays of a Humanist* (London: Penguin, 1964, reprint 1969), 82–83.

100 Cited from Vern Poythress, *Did Adam Exist?* (Phillipsburg, NJ: P&R, 2014), 5–7.

101 Ibid. 16.

102 Ibid. 19–28.

103 See earlier discussion on pages 80–83.

104 H. C. Leupold, *Exposition of Genesis, Volume 1: Chapters 1–19* (Grand Rapids, MI: Baker, 1942), 68.

105 For more evidence of this scientific failure, see Douglas F. Kelly, *Creation and Change* (Ross-shire, UK: Christian Focus, 1997), 195–199,

106 Peter Enns, *The Evolution of Adam* (Grand Rapids, MI: Brazos Press, 2012, 147.

107 Ibid.

Chapter 9.

108 G. Ch. Aalders, *Genesis*, 2 vols. (Grand Rapids, MI: Zondervan, 1981), 1:66.

109 Cited in R. Kent Hughes, *Genesis*, Preaching the Word (Wheaton, IL: Crossway, 2004), 32.

110 Cited from Charles Colson, "This Beautiful System—God's Handiwork in Space," *BreakPoint Commentary*, April 28, 1999.

111   Cited in Hughes, *Genesis*, 33.

112   Gordon J. Wenham, *Genesis 1–15*, Word Biblical Commentary (Dallas, TX: Word Books, 1987), 21.

113   John Currid, *Genesis: Volume 1, Genesis 1:1–25:18* (Darlington: UK: Evangelical Press, 2003), 76.

114   David Atkinson, *The Message of Genesis 1–11*, The Bible Speaks Today (Downers Grove, IL: InterVarsity, 1990), 32.

115   David Strasser and Richard Mullins, "Sometimes by Step," 1992.

Chapter 10.

116   Carl Sagan, *Pale Blue Dot* (New York, NY: Random House, 1994), 7.

117   See discussion on page 87.

118   John Calvin, *Sermons on Genesis Chapters 1–11*, trans. Rob Roy McGregor (Edinburgh: Banner of Truth, 2009),73

119   James Montgomery Boice, *Genesis*, 3 vols. (Grand Rapids, MI: Zondervan, 1982), 75.

120   Gordon J. Wenham, *Genesis 1–15*, Word Biblical Commentary (Dallas, TX: Word Books, 1987), 24.

121   Ibid.

122   Calvin, *Sermons on Genesis 1–11*, 81.

123   Ibid. 82.

124   David Wilkinson, *The Message of Creation*, The Bible Speaks Today (Downers Grove, IL: InterVarsity, 2002),28.

125   John Sailhamer, *Genesis*, in *The Expositor's Bible Commentary*, 12 volumes (Grand Rapids, MI, Zondervan, 1990), 2:54–55.

126 Bruce Waltke, *Genesis: A Commentary* (Grand Rapids, MI: Zondervan, 2001), 65.

127 Ibid.

128 Francis A. Schaeffer, *Genesis in Space and Time*, in *The Complete Works of Francis Schaeffer*, 5 vols. (Wheaton, IL: Crossway, 1985), 2:31.

129 Clyde T. Francisco, "Genesis," in *The Broadman Bible Commentary*, 12 vols. (Nashville, TN: Broadman, 1970), 1:125.

130 Howard Peskett & Vinoth Ramachandra, *The Message of Mission*, The Bible Speaks Today (Downers Grove, IL: InterVarsity, 2003), 36.

131 Gordon J. Wenham, *Genesis 1–15*, Word Biblical Commentary (Dallas, TX: Word Books, 1987), 30.

132 Schaeffer, *Genesis in Space and Time*, 2:33.

Chapter 11.

133 R. Kent Hughes, *Genesis*, Preaching the Word (Wheaton, IL: Crossway, 2004), 37.

134 Ibid.

135 John Calvin, *Sermons on Genesis Chapters 1–11*, trans. Rob Boy McGregor (Edinburgh: Banner of Truth, 2009), 93.

136 Alasdair Paine, *The First Chapters of Everything* (Ross-Shire, UK: Christian Focus, 2014), 54.

137 Philip Edgcumbe Hughes, *The True Image: The Origin and Destiny of Man in Christ* (Grand Rapids, MI: Eerdmans, 1989), 17

138 Cited from ibid. 53.

139 Victor Hamilton, *The Book of Genesis, Chapters 1–17*, New International Commentary on the Old Testament (Grand Rapids, MI: Eerdmans, 1990), 138.

140 Kenneth A. Mathews, *Genesis 1–11:26*, New American Commentary (Nashville, TN: B&H, 1996), 174.

141 *Westminster Confession of Faith*, 4.2.

142 Henri Blocher, *In the Beginning: The Opening Chapters of Genesis* (Leicester, UK: InterVarsity Press, 1984), 94.

143 Ibid.

144 Quoted from R. Kent Hughes, *John: That You May Believe* (Wheaton, IL: Crossway, 1999), 308.

Chapter 12.

145 Howard Peskett & Vinoth Ramachandra, *The Message of Mission*, The Bible Speaks Today (Downers Grove, IL: InterVarsity, 2003), 34–5.

146 "From his blood he formed mankind/imposed toil on man, set the gods free." Cited from Victor Hamilton, *The Books of Genesis, Chapters 1–17*, New International Commentary on the Old Testament (Grand Rapids, MI: Eerdmans, 1990), 140.

147 Gordon J. Wenham, *Genesis 1–15*, Word Biblical Commentary (Dallas, TX: Word Books, 1987), 33.

148 Ramachandra, *The Message of Mission*, 37.

149 Alasdair Paine, *The First Chapters of Everything* (Ross-Shire, UK: Christian Focus, 2014), 58.

150 Francis A. Schaeffer, *Death in the City* (Downers Grove, IL: InterVarsity, 1969), 80.

151 R. Albert Mohler, *We Cannot Be Silent* (Nashville, TN: Nelson, 2015), 17–22.

152 Ibid. 21.

153 Ramachandra, *The Message of Mission*, 50.

154 Paine, *The First Chapters of Everything*, 57.

155 Ramachandra, *The Message of Mission*, 49.

156 Isaac Watts, "Jesus Shall Reign," 1719.

Chapter 13.

157 David Wilkinson, *The Message of Creation*, The Bible Speaks Today (Downers Grove, IL: InterVarsity, 2002), 44.

158 John Calvin, *Genesis* (Edinburgh: Banner of Truth Trust, 1554, reprint 1992), 105.

159 G. K. Beale, *The Temple and the Church's Mission: A Biblical Theology of the Dwelling Place of God* (Downers Grove, IL: InterVarsity, 2004), 61.

160 John H. Walton, "Creation," in T. Desmond Alexander and David W. Baker, eds., *Dictionary of the Old Testament: Pentateuch* (Downers Grove, IL: InterVarsity, 2003), 161.

161 John H. Walton, *The Lost World of Genesis One: Ancient Cosmology and the Origins Debate* (Downers Grove, IL: IVP Academic, 2009), 74.

162 G. K. Beale, *A New Testament Theology* (Grand Rapids, MI: Baker, 2011), 800.

163 John G. Paton, *Missionary to the New Hebrides* (London: Hodder and Stoughton, 1891), 380.

164 John Calvin, *Genesis*, 106.